HARRY STYLES

THE BIOGRAPHY

HARRY STYLES

THE BIOGRAPHY

SARAH OLIVER

JB
JOHN BLAKE

Published by John Blake Publishing Ltd,
3 Bramber Court, 2 Bramber Road,
London W14 9PB, England

www.johnblakepublishing.co.uk

www.facebook.com/Johnblakepub facebook
twitter.com/johnblakepub twitter

First published in paperback in 2013

ISBN: 978 1 78219 220 6

British Library Cataloguing-in-Publication Data:

A catalogue record for this book is available from the British Library.

Printed and bound in Great Britain by CPI Group (UK) Ltd

Papers used by John Blake Publishing are natural, recyclable products made
from wood grown in sustainable forests. The manufacturing processes
conform to the environmental regulations of the country of origin.

Every attempt has been made to contact the relevant copyright-holders,
but some were unobtainable. We would be grateful if the
appropriate people could contact us.

DEDICATION

Dedicated with love to my husband Jon, Mum, Dad, Liz and Dan.

A big thank you to Harry's biggest fans: Abby Hulme, Carolina Fernandez-Bold, Abigail Fernandez-Bold, Melissa Seddon, Maryse Cantin, Lærke Visby, Macarena Sánchez, Fie Tegen Linde, Katrina Brooks and Josefine Olsen.

CONTENTS

If you love One Direction then you should follow the boys on Twitter. Here are their Twitter addresses:

One Direction – http://Twitter.com/onedirection
Harry – http://Twitter.com/harry_styles
Niall – https://Twitter.com/NiallOfficial
Zayn – https://Twitter.com/zaynmalik
Louis – https://Twitter.com/Louis_Tomlinson
Liam – https://Twitter.com/Real_Liam_Payne

Other interesting people connected to Harry, who you might want to follow:

One Direction's hairstylist, Lou Teasdale –
http://Twitter.com/louteasdale
Lou Teasdale's daughter – https://Twitter.com/Real_BabyLux
Harry's sister Gemma –
http://Twitter.com/GemmaAnneStyles
Harry's dad Des – https://Twitter.com/desstyles
Harry's mum Anne – https://Twitter.com/AnneFoxyCoxy
Harry's stepdad Robin – http://Twitter.com/robintwist
Harry's friends – http://Twitter.com/WillSweeny;
https://Twitter.com/ash_sherls

Harry's former band, White Eskimo –
http://Twitter.com/White_Eskimo
Harry's uncle – http://Twitter.com/Mike_Selley
Harry's auntie – http://Twitter.com/Dee_Selley
Harry's cousins – http://Twitter.com/matty_selley;
http://Twitter.com/concept_ben; http://Twitter.com/ella1d
Harry's cousin's band – http://Twitter.com/Conceptofficial
Dusty, Harry's cat – https://Twitter.com/DustyDaCat

Harry Styles is the youngest member of One Direction and has the most Twitter followers. He is the most popular member in the UK, but Niall Horan is the most popular in the USA. To contact Harry, or another member of One Direction, write to: The Matrix Complex, 91 Peterborough Road, London, SW6 3BU.

CHAPTER 1

1994: A STAR IS BORN!

Harry Edward Styles was born on 1 February 1994 and was affectionately given the nickname 'H' by his family. His mum Anne and dad Des were overjoyed to have a little boy, and his sister Gemma was glad to have a little playmate. They lived in Evesham, Worcestershire, but moved to Holmes Chapel in Cheshire when he was a baby. Harry's dad Des is originally from Peterborough.

Harry attended Happy Days Club & Nursery School, and he can still remember the fun he had there. He was a happy child, always laughing and joking, rarely crying. His mum worked in an office and his dad worked for financial corporations in their Operations departments, but he is now the sales and marketing director for a company in Blackburn.

When he was four Harry left nursery and went to Hermitage Primary School, in Holmes Chapel. He made some good friends there, including a boy called Jonathan who is still his friend today. Every year they put on a play at Christmas, with all the children in the school taking part. Some just sang in the choir but Harry enjoyed acting, so he was given big roles. He played the lead one year, as a mouse called Barney, and you can see a video of him performing on YouTube if you search 'Harry Styles before he was famous'. Harry looks so cute standing on the stage on his own wearing a grey sweater and tights. He wore a long tail that trailed on the floor and mouse ears on his head. He had to do the actions while the rest of the children in his school sang a song about him. In another play, he had to dress up as Buzz Lightyear and pretend to be a toy.

DID YOU KNOW?

Harry admitted in an interview with *KansasCity.com* that he had been bullied when he was five or six years old. He said: 'I think the most important thing is to make sure you tell somebody. Make sure you talk to your parents or let somebody know.'

Harry left a lasting impression on his teachers, and in their autumn 2010 newsletter they wrote: 'We all remember Harry for a fantastic performance as the Pharaoh ("Elvis") in *Joseph and the Amazing Technicolour Dreamcoat* in Year 6. He certainly brought his own "style" to the role!'

While Harry was at Hermitage Primary School his parents broke up. He was only seven at the time and it really upset him. His dad Des can still remember Harry crying as he told him the news; it's something he will never forget. He hated hurting Harry and Gemma. They wanted their parents to stay together but that was impossible, and Des and Anne broke the news to them in the living room of their home. Des lived with them for two more years but eventually left; Anne took Harry and Gemma and moved to the countryside, becoming the landlady of a pub with a new partner. Des didn't like the man but when she started to date Robin, who is now Harry's stepdad, he approved because he thought Robin was a nice bloke. Harry was about 12 when his mum began seeing Robin and they had moved back to Holmes Chapel by then.

Des told the *Daily Record*: 'Of course, I missed him [Harry] and Gemma, as you would unless you were some sort of monster. It was tough. I used to feed him every night at half 10, change his nappy, put him to bed when he was a baby, and then I was no longer living with them.'

Des only saw Harry every two weeks once he had left, but he gave Anne money towards the children's upkeep. Harry and Des have a good relationship, with Des telling the newspaper: 'I'm not an estranged dad. It was a tough time to leave them but these things happen.'

Anne gave Harry a fantastic childhood and Des credits her with the way Harry turned out. Harry had some amazing holidays when he was younger, both when his dad was with them and after his parents had separated. He can still remember when he went with his family to Disney World and the strange dreams he had back then – he used to dream that rats had eaten his toes. He can also remember going ice skating and keeping a tight grip on the sides so that he didn't fall.

Harry started acting and performing at primary school, and confessed to the *X Factor* backstage cameras: 'The first time I sang properly was in a school production – the rush that I got was something that I really enjoyed and wanted to do more of.'

Harry doesn't come from a musical family as such but his dad loves Elvis, and Harry would sing along to his Elvis tapes when he was growing up. Harry has never been shy and when his granddad gave him a karaoke machine he had great fun pretending to be a singer. As well as singing he loved sport and was a goalie for the

Holmes Chapel Hurricanes Football team. They wore red and black kits and Harry was popular with his teammates.

When he was 11, Harry left Hermitage Primary School and went to Holmes Chapel Comprehensive School; he already knew a lot of people there because of playing in the football team. He made lots of new friends as well as having the friends he had had in primary school. At break times he would have a laugh with his friends. One day, 10 of them decided to build a human pyramid. There were four lads on the bottom kneeling down, then three on top of them, then two (including Harry) and one balanced on the top. Another friend quickly took a photo before they collapsed in a heap.

At that time, Harry used to wear quite a few bracelets on his wrists, which made him stand out from the crowd; he wore a navy polo shirt with the school crest for PE, and a white polo shirt with a black sweater for the rest of the time.

DID YOU KNOW?

Harry didn't always have curly hair; he went through a phase of having his hair straight while at school. When he was still in primary school he had blond streaks added – he thought he looked great but looking back, he's no longer so convinced. He prefers his hair as it is now.

Harry is still in touch with a lot of his friends from school and from growing up in Holmes Chapel. His best lad mates are Will, Jon, Nick and Ben and his best girl mates are Ashley, Naomi, Emilie, Ellis, Lydia and Sophie. Harry was popular with the girls at school – not because they wanted to date him but because he was a genuinely nice guy. He did date his friend Emilie for a while, though, when they were 12, and had another girlfriend called Abi.

Harry really enjoyed his English classes and went on lots of trips to see the musical *Blood Brothers* and the play *The Woman in Black*. A straight-A student, Harry was very talented at sport, too. He is a quick learner and is especially good at badminton, football and cricket.

Harry used to have loads of fun with his friends. When he was 14, during a school trip to Paris, they were messing around and Harry threw a cake in his friend's face for a laugh. Another time they wrapped him in cling film (plastic wrap) so he couldn't walk, he just had to hop; on another day they put makeup on him when he was fast asleep and they also filmed a video of him singing the song 'Look After You' upside down, with eyes and a nose drawn onto his chin. And one night, Harry nearly got into trouble with his friend's mum, as he explained to *We Love Pop* magazine: 'At my friend's birthday party a few years ago I got dared to go and get in bed with his mum. She was asleep and she woke up when I got in, so I just ran back down the stairs.'

Harry's school prom was held at Portal Golf Club, Tarporley and he looked dashing in his suit with a pink flower in his buttonhole. He posed for photos with lots of his female friends.

Harry joined a band when he was in Year 8 (12/13 years old). His best friend Will and another friend Hayden were the original members of the band that was to become White Eskimo; they practised at Will's house because he had a drum kit and his family didn't mind them making lots of noise. Will and Hayden thought they needed a bass player and singer if they were to become a proper band, so Will asked Harry if he wanted to learn the bass. Harry said he would, but then Will found out their other friend Nick could already play bass so he had experience. Will still wanted Harry to be in the band and so he suggested that he should sing instead. Harry told him, 'No, I can't sing', but Will convinced him to give it a go. Harry didn't think he was good enough because he'd only ever sung in the shower before but it turned out he was actually very good. In their practice sessions Harry would play the kazoo and the tambourine during some songs.

They didn't have a name but needed one as they wanted to enter a 'Battle of the Bands' competition at school. Harry came up with the perfect name – White Eskimo. It didn't mean anything; it was just something random that popped into his head. They were influenced by rock bands rather than boy bands and would listen to tracks by blink-182, You Me At Six, Paramore, +44, Travis Barker, Kings of Leon, The Offspring, Green Day and Jimmy Eat World.

The band's first performance was in their school canteen on 2 July 2009. Keen to do well in the Battle of the Bands competition, they had rehearsed lots and picked songs that they thought people would like. They performed the Bryan Adams' classic 'Summer of '69' and 'Are You Gonna Be My Girl?' by the rock band Jet. The songs went down a storm: people were cheering and taking photos, they couldn't get enough. Harry looked gorgeous; he was wearing a white shirt with a black tie, grey trousers and a large tan-coloured belt. The bandmates were so happy when they found out they'd won, especially as they hadn't been together for long at all.

Winning the competition had a big impact on Harry, as he later revealed to X Factor host Dermot O'Leary in his first interview: 'Winning Battle of the Bands and playing in front of that many people really showed me that's what I wanted to do. I got such a thrill when I was in front of people singing, it made me want to do more and more.'

After they'd won, White Eskimo performed at lots of school assemblies, and even a wedding. If you want to see some of their performances just type 'White Eskimo' into YouTube. You can see them perform 'First Date' by blink-182, 'Valerie' by The Zutons, 'Jenny Don't Be Hasty' by Paolo Nutini and 'A Hard Day's Night' by The Beatles. Altogether they performed more than 30 different songs and it's a shame more of them aren't on YouTube.

DID YOU KNOW?

Will is still Harry's best friend, even though Harry is really close to Louis Tomlinson. He never actually officially left White Eskimo, so if he ever wanted to rejoin for a one-off gig they'd let him. Today the White Eskimo line-up consists of Will [Sweeny] on vocals, Josh Clarke on guitar, Sam Greenwood on bass and Alex Lewis on drums. Check out their fan page on Facebook or follow them on Twitter: http://Twitter.com/White_Eskimo.

White Eskimo have their own manager now and have been gigging around the UK. They have recorded some great tracks in a London studio and worked with the music producer Jon Kelly, who has worked with Kate Bush, The Beautiful South and Paul McCartney.

As well as having good friends like Will to talk to, Harry is very close to his big sister Gemma, but they did have their fair share of arguments while growing up. Gemma used to get really irritated when Harry put on silly voices and didn't find it funny at all. Their first pet was a dog called Max and they had a hamster – called hamster – but they now have a black-and-white cat called Dusty, who has over 30,000 fans on Twitter. Harry admits that he's more of a cat person than a dog person. His family have never bought a pet; they always adopt from rescue centres or take in pets no one else wants.

Gemma is currently studying for a degree at Sheffield University. You can tell by looking at her that she's Harry's sister as they share some characteristics, but her hair is poker straight, whereas Harry's is curly. No one in the family knows where Harry got his curls from as his dad Des has really short hair and mum Anne has wavy hair. Harry's mum used to love her son's hair when he was little, telling *Star Magazine*: 'It was white blond with curls at the end when he was younger, but we had it cut because he looked a bit too pretty!'

Both Gemma and Anne tweet all the time, so it is worth following them on Twitter as you will get to see the tweets they send to Harry. They are both so proud of him, and love him so much. Check out their Twitter accounts at the front of the book.

When he turned 16 on 1 February 2010, Harry hadn't sat his GCSEs (final exams) but he had to decide what he wanted to do in life. Aside from school, he was working in a local bakery but his dream job was to be a singer. He was going to do A-levels in law, sociology and business, but after encouragement from his mum he decided to apply for *The X Factor* first to see whether he had what it takes to be world-class singer. (His mum was actually the one who filled out the form!) The minimum age for entry was 16 and as the auditions were taking place in June and July, Harry was only just eligible. If unsuccessful, he had thoughts of becoming a lawyer or a sports physiotherapist. He had no idea how much his life was about to change.

DID YOU KNOW?

On Tuesday, 24 August 2010 Harry went to school to pick up his GCSE results but he didn't stick around. He found out that he'd passed all 12 of his subjects, but he didn't reveal the actual scores; he kept them private. His local paper printed all the results for his school and revealed that he got 12, graded between A$\star$ and C.

CHAPTER 2

TIME TO SHINE

Harry auditioned for *The X Factor* in Manchester, just like Louis Tomlinson, but they didn't meet that day. His friend Will went with Harry and his mum to his very first audition. They queued up at 6am in Trafford, Manchester and had to wait for hours and hours. Will could tell Harry was very excited but nervous at the same time. He really hoped his friend would get through. The *X Factor* production team thought that Harry had great potential so he was interviewed by Dermot O'Leary. For his audition Harry wore a white T-shirt with a grey cardigan and a green and black scarf. He chose casual trousers rather than jeans and looked quite smart without being over the top.

For *The X Factor* the singers don't get to go in front of the judges straight away; they have to impress in several rounds first before coming back another day. The people behind the scenes only let the very best and the very worst singers through. When Harry's friends and family found out that he was good enough to go in front of Simon Cowell and the other judges they couldn't wait. They had special T-shirts printed with 'We Think Harry Has The X Factor' printed on them; the women wore white ones and the men had black versions to make themselves stand out from the crowd and let Harry know they were behind him 100 per cent.

For Harry, getting the opportunity to audition was a dream come true. He had wanted to audition for the show in previous years but had been too young. Harry told Dermot O'Leary in his first *X Factor* interview: 'People tell me I'm a good singer – it's usually my mum [pointing to Anne, who was standing right next to him]. Singing is what I want to do!'

When he was called to go on stage, Anne was so emotional that she gave him a kiss on his cheek; his cousin gave him a kiss on his head. Gemma gave him a good-luck pat on the back too. Dermot jokingly asked the rest of his friends and family if anyone else wanted to kiss him!

Harry might have been nervous but the audience loved him straight away. He didn't even have to start singing – they just started to cheer. He had picked Stevie Wonder's 'Isn't She Lovely' for his audition song, an unusual choice for someone of his age. By the time he'd finished, Harry had the audience spellbound – and guest judge Nicole Scherzinger was totally smitten. Behind the scenes, his family were applauding and his mum punched the air in delight. She knew he'd put in an amazing performance.

What the judges said:

Nicole Scherzinger: 'I'm really glad that we had the opportunity to hear you a cappella 'cos we could really hear how great your voice is. For 16 years old, you have a beautiful voice.'

Louis Walsh: 'I agree with Nicole... however, I think you're so young. I don't think you have enough experience or confidence yet.'

Simon Cowell [talking to Louis]: 'Someone in the audience just said "rubbish" and I totally agree with them because the show is designed to find someone, whether you're 15, 16, 17, it doesn't matter. I think with a bit of vocal coaching, you actually could be very good.'

When it came to casting votes, Louis said: 'Harry, for all the right reasons I am going to say no.' Meanwhile, Simon Cowell was so disgusted with Louis' rejection that he encouraged the audience to boo him louder – even Harry joined in with a 'boo'. Nicole confessed, 'I like you, Harry, I'm going to say yes' and then Simon added, 'You'll be happy to hear that I'm going to be agreeing with Nicole.' Harry was so thrilled to be going through that he was a bit speechless and just said, 'Thank you... cheers, thanks', and walked offstage to be given a huge hug by his mum.

DID YOU KNOW?

Harry's audition number was 165998, Louis' was 155204, Zayn's was 165616, Liam's was 61898 and Niall's was 232677.

Anne was so proud of him but she couldn't tell her friends that her son had made it through to bootcamp until the audition was shown on TV months later, in September.

DID YOU KNOW?

If you try to find Harry on Facebook you won't be able to find him because he had to delete his account once his *X Factor* audition had been shown on TV. He did try to set up a secret account after the band started touring but ended up having to delete that as well because fans and journalists found out. He doesn't mind sharing things on Twitter but he wanted to have a private Facebook page so that he could just be Harry from Holmes Chapel and chat to his old mates. He might try again in the future and only tell a handful of people about it.

Harry might have impressed at his first audition but he knew he had to raise his game at the bootcamp stage if he was going to progress. More than 200 people had made it through to the bootcamp round, which was held at Wembley Arena in London over five days in July 2010.

Harry arrived nice and early on the morning of 22 July; he couldn't afford to be late because he had to register and then prepare for the first challenge. On arrival, he was told to stand with the other boys who had made it through as the judges wanted everyone in four categories: Boys, Girls, Over-25s and Groups. Harry didn't have a clue about his closest competition; up until that point none of their first auditions had been aired on TV. It must have been quite isolating because he didn't have his family and friends there to support him.

Harry and the rest of the boys were told to rehearse Michael Jackson's 'Man In The Mirror', the girls were given Beyoncé's track, 'If I Were A Boy', the over-25s sang Lady Gaga's 'Poker Face' and the groups were given 'Nothing's Gonna Stop Us Now' by Starship. All of the singers knew they had to come up with their own interpretation of the song, or risk Simon telling them they were karaoke singers or just mimicking the original artists.

Harry must have felt under so much pressure when Simon said, 'By the end of the day, half of you are going home. Today, you're going to be put in your categories and you're going to sing one song. There are literally no second chances today.' Harry didn't want to return to Holmes Chapel early, he didn't want his dreams to be over.

For the first challenge, Simon was going to be judging them alongside Louis Walsh. Louis had already said that he felt Harry was too young and had said no in his first audition. Now Harry had to do his best to blow him away and make him change his mind otherwise it could all be over.

In forcing everyone to sing the same song, Simon was putting them under pressure to see who was good enough – he wanted them to be able to learn the words off by heart, and put in an amazing performance on top of that. In the past Harry had learnt lots of songs by heart for White Eskimo but they had been mostly rock songs. Some of the stronger singers from the first auditions couldn't cope under the pressure and failed to sing in tune or remember the lines. Dermot O'Leary was shocked that some of those singers had no idea how badly they had done and would talk to him afterwards as if they had nailed it. Harry wasn't one of them, he had put in a solid performance, and Dermot must have been impressed. After being told that he had made it through to Bootcamp Day Two, Harry was so relieved.

Harry and some of the other contestants had a bit of a celebration that night but Harry didn't stay up too late; he needed to be fresh for the morning. As soon as he arrived at Wembley the next day he was told to go on the stage with the other singers. Simon and Louis then revealed a twist: they were going to be taught how to dance by one of the best choreographers in the business, Brian Friedman. Brian has worked with Britney Spears, Beyoncé Knowles, Usher, Mariah Carey and many more top artists, so Harry and the rest of the singers felt very privileged.

Brian wanted to reassure the contestants. 'I don't want you to be scared,' he told them. 'What we are going to work on is your stage presence and choreography.' Simon just wanted to see how the singers handled the challenge he had set them and he wasn't going to eliminate someone if they were not very good at dancing; he just wanted to see them give it a try. Harry was keen to learn and picked the routine up quite quickly, laughing and joking behind the scenes. He had never had dance lessons before but you couldn't tell because he moved so well. If you want to see him practising, go on YouTube and search 'Harry Styles dancing at bootcamp'.

Harry hadn't properly met Liam, Louis, Niall or Zayn at this point, but he did stand behind Zayn during their performance in front of the judges. Zayn was a lot less confident and had initially refused to dance because he didn't want to look like an idiot on TV. Simon had gone behind the scenes and convinced him to give it a go, telling him he would regret it if he didn't at least try. It's a good job Zayn took Simon's advice: One Direction might have been made up of four members instead of five.

Although Harry was doing well, he was conscious that his dream could be over any minute. 'As you go through bootcamp you kind of realise how big the prize is,' he explained during a backstage interview. 'So being here the last few days has made me realise how much I wanna stay – I really don't want to go home now.'

Simon and Louis were joined by a third judge on the third

day: former Pussycat Dolls' singer Nicole Scherzinger. She was replacing Cheryl Cole, who was recovering from malaria and had been too ill to attend bootcamp for the first two days. Nicole had been impressed with Harry when he sang 'Isn't She Lovely' in the first audition, so he must have been excited to see her back. However, Nicole might have liked Harry first time around but he was going to have to impress her even more if he was to get through to the judges' houses round; there were so many talented singers still left in the competition.

Harry and the rest of the contestants had been expecting to perform in front of a live audience in the final days of bootcamp, but X Factor producers decided that because Cheryl wasn't going to be there they would cancel the live element of the bootcamp week. They tweeted on the official X Factor Twitter: 'Due to the unusual circumstances, we are not inviting an audience to watch the contestants perform at The X Factor bootcamp.' Thousands of fans were gutted as they'd been looking forward to seeing the performances. This must have been disappointing for Harry, too, because he loves performing in front of a crowd, and had been boosted by their cheers before he started singing at his first audition.

Harry and the rest of the contestants had 40 songs to choose from for their last performance at bootcamp, and they had been practising hard since the third day. Everyone wanted to choose the perfect song for themselves, which was a big test – they didn't want to go for something that lots of other people would pick, or something that wasn't challenging enough. Harry chose 'Stop Crying Your Heart Out' by Oasis. He didn't know it at the time but Liam had chosen the same song! Sadly Harry's performance was never shown on TV, so fans can only see Liam perform his version on YouTube.

The final, fifth day of bootcamp was the most nerve-wracking for the surviving contestants. They had seen so many people leave the competition and were dreading the moment when they would be called onstage. The vast majority felt sick and had hardly slept; they just had to wait and see who Simon, Nicole and Louis decided to put through. The judges were going to take their time and make sure they got it right, so it meant waiting around for hours.

In previous series of *The X Factor* the judges put six acts in each category through to the judges' houses round, but for the 2010 series they decided to put through a total of 32 (eight in each category). This was good news for Harry as he had more chance of getting through.

Nicole, Simon and Louis had such a hard task ahead of them; the standard was so high that they decided to increase the age of the over-25s category so that it became the over-28s. They thought that by doing this the talented 20-somethings could be more evenly spread out. This meant that Harry was up against more people than he originally thought, and there were now 30 remaining boys (including himself).

By the time the boys were called onto the stage tensions were running high. No one wanted to go home but they knew that 22 of them would be. Simon started by calling out the first name. Harry must have felt sick to the stomach, desperate for his name to be called out.

Simon announced: 'The first person through to the judges' houses is… John Wilding.'

Nicole was next: 'Nicolo Festa.'

Then Louis: 'Paije Richardson.'

Simon: 'Aiden Grimshaw.'

Louis: 'Marlon McKenzie.'

Louis: 'Karl Brown.'

Nicole: 'Matt Cardle.'

With one final place up for grabs Harry's heart must have been beating so fast.

Simon: 'The final contestant who's made it through is Tom Richards. That's it, guys – I'm really sorry.'

The 22 boys who hadn't made it walked offstage. Harry was devastated, thinking that his hard work over the week was all for nothing. 'I'm really gutted,' he cried into his hat. Liam was welling up, telling Dermot O'Leary, 'I just don't want to go home, I just don't want to go.' Niall was inconsolable, telling the camera, 'Standing there, waiting for your name to be called – and then it's not.' Harry hid his face under his sweater and moved away from the camera; he didn't want to talk any more.

The boys got ready to leave, but before they could go a member of staff came and called our five favourite lads back. Harry covered his face in shock, thinking that maybe things weren't over after all. They were asked to go back on the stage with Esther Campbell, Rebecca Creighton, Sophia Wardman and Geneva Lane. None of them knew what was happening, but they didn't have long to wait. Nicole spoke first, saying, 'Hello, thank you so much for coming back. Judging from some of your faces, this is really hard. We've thought long and hard about it, and we've thought of each of you as individuals, and we just feel that you're too talented to let go of. We think it would be a great idea to have two separate groups.'

Simon then suggested that they should form groups and might meet again in the future, before adding, 'We've decided to put you both through. This is a lifeline – you've got to work 10, 12, 14 hours a day, every single day, and take this opportunity. You've got a real shot here, guys.'

Up until then, Harry and the rest of the boys had been thinking that the judges wanted them to re-audition the following year. Getting a pass to the judges' houses round was unbelievable, as they hadn't even sung together yet. They had to decide, though, whether they wanted to become a band, as they'd all wanted to be solo artists to begin with.

Harry knew straight away that he wanted to do it; after all, he'd been with White Eskimo and knew that performing with others was great fun. Liam wasn't sure and wanted to think about it first. After a quick think, he said yes, he was going to give it his all. Zayn, Niall and Louis were all up for it, too, and they weren't going to let Simon, Nicole and Louis down. They were going to be the best group ever to appear on *The X Factor*.

DID YOU KNOW?

Before entering *The X Factor* Louis had posted a forum online to see if anyone fancied forming a band and then entering *The X Factor* but no one had replied, so he decided to go for it anyway, as a solo artist.

DID YOU KNOW?

One Direction was officially formed on 23 July 2010 at 8.22pm.

Harry admitted: '[I went from] the worst feeling in my life to the best.'

As he walked into the room with all the other singers who had been chosen for the next round, Harry was so happy. He gave his bootcamp buddy Aiden Grimshaw the biggest hug!

The bootcamp episodes weren't shown on TV until the October, so his family had a while to wait to see them on TV. Harry's mum decided to throw a bootcamp party when it aired. Harry had never danced before his audition for *The X*

Factor, so his family were impressed when they saw how well he had stepped up to the dance challenge. 'I fill up with pride every time he's on TV,' Anne told the *Crewe Chronicle*. 'I feel incredibly proud and it's all so surreal to see my boy on the stage. At the end of the day, he's my little baby and there he is, onstage in front of millions of people.'

Anne wasn't the only proud one – right from when his first audition was shown on TV, people from his home village of Holmes Chapel showed their immense pride by supporting him in every way they could. In his first *X Factor* video Harry described Holmes Chapel as being 'quite boring... nothing much happens there – it's quite picturesque.' His neighbours didn't mind that he had said where they lived was dull, because they love how quiet it is. Shopkeepers and home owners put up 'Go Harry' and 'Vote One Direction' posters in their windows; they wanted all 6,000 Holmes Chapel residents to vote for him. The W Mandeville bakery where Harry used to work had One Direction loaves and cakes on display, and Anne even bought some cakes from there to give to Simon and Dermot. When he worked in the bakery, Harry's job was to clean the floor at night and serve customers on a Saturday. His former boss Simon Wakefield was interviewed by the local newspaper. 'He's welcome back any time but I highly doubt he'll be back to work,' he told the *Crewe Chronicle*. 'I think his career is sorted. He is a great lad and was really popular with the customers when he used to work on the counter.'

One Direction fans loved the fact that Harry used to work in a bakery and a Facebook page called 'Harry Styles works in a bakery. I would check out his buns every day' was set up. To date, it has more than 12,000 members.

DID YOU KNOW?

Before Harry worked in the bakery he had a newspaper round. He blames his bad posture on the heavy bag of papers he used to carry over his shoulder but he used to love riding his bike, so it was a good job at the time. After joining One Direction he was advised to take up Pilates once a week to help improve his posture but he is so busy he really doesn't have the time.

One Direction (or the 'unnamed boys' group – because they didn't have a name at this point) didn't know who their mentor was going to be when they left bootcamp. It could have been Simon Cowell, Louis Walsh, Cheryl Cole or Dannii Minogue (the judges themselves didn't know because it was down to the show's producers to decide). Shortly after bootcamp, the judges found out who would be mentoring each category. They were each in a different country when they got the phone call revealing their fate: Simon was in England, Louis in Ireland, Cheryl in America and Dannii was in Australia. Simon ideally wanted the 'girls' because he thought they were the strongest category, followed by the 'boys'. When told that he would be mentoring the 'groups', he wasn't at all happy and asked the producer to repeat what he had said, before replying sarcastically, 'Thank you for repaying all of my hard work on the show this year.'

Harry and the boys had no idea that Simon thought that the groups weren't as good as the boys and girls at this point. They were just excited about the fact that if they got through to the live shows they would get to work with arguably the biggest man in the music industry.

From the second they became a group on 23 July, the boys

vowed to work together to make sure they made the live shows. In previous years, the groups formed by the judges had been hopeless, blaming lack of rehearsal time when criticised for not performing well enough. Harry and the boys knew they wouldn't be able to impress Simon if they didn't give it their all. They arranged to meet at Harry's house in Holmes Chapel, a few days after bootcamp, which gave them just enough time to go home and pack a suitcase before heading off. It was the summer, so it was easy to make excuses if they needed to; they could just tell their friends they were going on holiday, and they weren't missing school or college so they couldn't get in trouble.

As well as practising they had to come up with a unique name that they all liked; they couldn't turn up at Simon's house without one. They thought of some ideas and texted each other while they were back at their own homes. Harry came up with the name One Direction, as he explained during an interview on an Australian chat show: 'Before we met up for the time to practise, we were texting each other names constantly. I kind of thought what would sound good when the *X Factor* man said it. So, then I texted the boys and they all seemed to like it.'

They stayed at Harry's house for a week, getting to know each other and rehearsing; then went home for a few days (so their mums could wash their clothes!) and came back for more rehearsals. Altogether they spent nearly three weeks rehearsing, day and night (and doing fun stuff too, of course). The lads got to see the best and worst parts of each other during those three weeks. They slept in a bungalow, which is at the bottom of the main house's garden. It has its own swimming pool, which the boys took full advantage of during their stay. They also went to one of Harry's favourite places – Great Budworth Ice Cream Farm, run by the Wilkinson family. The farm offers traditional flavours such as vanilla, strawberry and chocolate, and more unusual ones like marzipan, pineapple and Christmas pudding. If you go to the Great Budworth Ice Cream Farm Facebook page you can see a great album of photos of One Direction enjoying some ice creams, but it was a cold day so they're wrapped up to keep warm. There's even a photo of Harry pretending to work there!

During their stay, the boys managed to damage one of the chairs in Harry's mum's house, and during an interview with Radio 1, Anne asked if they could find out from the band who had broken it. 'They'd sit out in the garden, around the fire pit and the chairs,' she explained. 'Just chilling and generally getting to know each other and cracking on with some work really and breaking chair legs!'

The boys had some petty squabbles in those few weeks, which was to be expected really because they were with each other 24 hours a day, near enough. They had entered the competition as solo artists, with different musical influences, and so they had different ideas about the kind of group they wanted to be. It was really tricky trying to decide who should sing lead vocals and who would take care of the harmonies. They would have all liked to be the lead singer but that wasn't possible, so they had to think carefully. Each of them tried out and, after many practices and discussions, found their place in the group.

For Harry and the boys, being onstage and performing was really important and they didn't want their *X Factor* journey to come to an end. Liam told *X Factor* cameras months later during the live shows, 'Being on stage is absolutely amazing! I mean, we only spend such a short time on it but we love absolutely every second of it. We wouldn't change any of it, it's great!'

Zayn admitted on the *X Factor* website, 'This for us is just unbelievable! We were all sat in the car today and I think it was

Liam that said, "It feels like a dream and that we're all going to wake up and our mums are gonna be like, 'Wake up, get ready for school!' kind of thing.'"

'I think it's easy for people at home to look at us and think we're just having fun,' Louis continued. 'The reason we're having fun is because we're working hard.'

DID YOU KNOW?

Before a performance the boys like to get in a huddle, wish each other good luck and share some private jokes. They drink water or energy drinks and Niall likes to have some lemon and ginger tea. Liam likes to do a few press-ups to focus himself and Zayn used to brush his teeth but he doesn't do it as much anymore. Niall would change his socks and Harry would change his pants.

Harry found out pretty early on that he had much in common with Louis and they became great friends. The boys all have different personalities and have come from all corners of England and Ireland, but everyone gets on. They each bring something different to the group. If Louis had to describe the other members in one word he would pick 'flirty' for Harry, 'smart' for Liam, 'vain' for Zayn and 'funny' for Niall. Harry would pick 'leader' for Louis.

In an interview with the *Shropshire Star*, Liam said, 'The dynamic of our band is that there are loud people and there are quiet people, and there are people in between – I would say I am probably one of the in-between people and one of the quiet people. But we all get on so well, it's unbelievable. Everyone is just so happy to be here, we just have a laugh, 24/7. It is hard to get to sleep at night – everyone just carries on joking about.'

Louis told *Digital Spy* what happens when they have disagreements. 'Because we're around each other so often it's like arguing with your siblings,' he confessed. 'You fall out with them, go away and have a bit of a paddy, then come back and get over it.'

Liam added, 'I think every band has arguments but the funny thing is, you just get over them really quickly – they last about five minutes. You just get over it because you know we're all going for the same thing so you just put your differences aside and get on with it.'

Harry thinks they will never have an argument big enough to split them up because they are all such good friends, they only argue over petty things.

DID YOU KNOW?

If Zayn ever causes an argument, he treats them all to a takeaway to make up for it!

CHAPTER 3

IMPRESSING SIMON

After rehearsing for three weeks, some people might think that flying out to Spain was a treat for the boys – but they weren't going on holiday. The flight was nerve-wracking, but exciting at the same time. They had put so much time into turning themselves into a group but they knew that the seven other groups flying out with them were all desperate for a place in *The X Factor* finals, too.

The lads couldn't get over how luxurious Simon's rented villa in Marbella was; it had an incredible 20 bedrooms, a home cinema and three swimming pools. They didn't let it distract them from what they were doing, though; they had come to Spain to put on an amazing performance and they only had one chance to impress Simon with the song he had picked out for them.

Harry and the boys were aware that Simon would be looking for the whole package, so they needed to look good. They had combined their individual styles to create a unified look that complemented each member, with all of them wearing grey or white pumps, casual three-quarter length trousers or shorts and loose-fitting shirts or T-shirts. Their clothes were a combination of blue, white and brown; no one stood out in bright colours. Harry wore a scarf and Niall had a buttoned-up shirt, just as in their first auditions. (Poor Louis had a sore foot after being stung by a sea urchin and so he ended up wearing flip-flops for the performance!)

When Louis was stung while they were at the beach, he was rushed to hospital, leaving Harry and the others to rehearse on their own. They had no idea whether he would be back in time for their performance in front of Simon, so they had to consider that it might just be the four of them. 'We're all panicking a little bit 'cos we're not sure what's going to happen or when he's going to get here,' Zayn admitted to the *X Factor* cameras that day. Liam added: 'For us that's really bad as we haven't had that much time to practise as we've only just got together as a group. I hope he's back as we really do need him.'

Of course Harry and the others would have been able to put in a performance without Louis but it wouldn't have been as good. Thankfully, he was dropped off at the villa just in time. The boys rushed over to their bandmate and gave him a big hug before carrying him inside. Together they walked confidently to the performing area, which was by one of the swimming pools. Simon was seated under a parasol with former 80s pop star Sinitta. She was helping him to choose the acts that he should put through to the live shows. The reunited five-piece performed the Natalie Imbruglia classic 'Torn': Liam sang the first verse brilliantly and then Harry nailed the chorus.

Niall and Louis harmonised perfectly and Zayn finished off. It was a group effort, but each one performed wonderfully; it was as though they'd been singing together forever.

As soon as they'd finished, Simon said thanks and they walked off, thanking the guitarist and keyboard player as they passed them. Once they'd gone, Simon told his helper Sinitta, 'They're cool, they're relevant.' He could tell they'd been a bit nervous but he'd been impressed with how well they'd sung.

Harry summed up how they were all feeling, telling the camera: 'Your hunger for it grows and grows as you get through each stage in the competition. It's just the biggest stage to be told "yes" or "no"... it's one word that can change your life forever because it won't be the same if you get a "yes", and if you get a "no", then it's straight back to doing stuff that kind of drives you to come here in the first place.'

★ ★ ★

Here are the groups One Direction were competing against and the songs Simon chose for them to sing:

Husstle sang 'Tainted Love' by Soft Cell

The Reason sang Daniel Bedingfield's 'If You're Not The One'

FYD sang 'Beggin'' by Madcon

Diva Fever sang 'Love Machine' by Girls Aloud

Twem sang Kelly Rowland's 'When Love Takes Over'

Belle Amie sang George Michael's 'Faith'

Princes & Rogues sang 'Video Killed The Radio Star'

Some of the groups who had been favourites to go through didn't impress Simon and Sinitta in their performances, whereas others, like One Direction, had excelled. Picking the top three to go through was very difficult.

After considering the options, Simon made his final decision and called in each group, one at a time, to let them know whether they would be going to the live shows or going home. When it was One Direction's turn, Harry led the way, with the others following behind him. They all lined up next to each other, their arms around each other's shoulders for support and in a sign of unity. 'Do you understand why I did this in the first place?' Simon asked. 'Yes,' they replied. 'I think it's because once we got through to the bootcamp stage, there were weaknesses, which is why we made the decision about all of you individually,' he continued. 'To a point, you came in at a disadvantage because you didn't have the time the other groups had. On the more positive note, when it works, it worked.

'My head is saying it's a risk and my heart is saying that you deserve a shot. And that's why it's been difficult. So I've made a decision, guys – I've gone with my heart, you're through!'

The boys started screaming and then had a massive group hug. They had done it! Harry couldn't contain his excitement and leaving the others, ran over to hug Simon, closely followed by Niall and Zayn, Louis and Liam; Harry even had tears in his eyes again, only this time they were tears of happiness rather than rejection. Simon told them, 'I am so impressed with all of you; I mean that.'

The boys were so excited, but they had to take care not to upset the groups who had just been told they weren't good enough and were going home. Harry couldn't wait to ring and tell his excited family the good news: they were going to be performing every Saturday night, with 11 million people watching at home! They were one step closer to landing a recording deal.

CHAPTER 4

THE NEXT STEP

The boys could briefly go home to see their families but then they had to be back in London so they could prepare for the first live show. Everything was still under wraps because the judges' houses TV episodes hadn't been shown and the media were desperate to know who was through – but if people found out it would ruin the surprise. Harry's mum loaned him some money so that he could buy some new clothes, as the *X Factor* camera crew were going to be following them every day and he didn't have enough of a wardrobe. He'd been used to wearing school uniform Monday to Friday, and some of his clothes weren't suitable for a budding pop star.

For the actual live shows the boys had stylists, who would fill a rack with suitable garments for them, and Harry could choose whatever he wanted to wear. He picked clothes that matched what the others were wearing but at the same time showed off his personality. Sometimes the bandmates would choose their own clothes but during the final rehearsals the stylists or someone else from the *X Factor* team would say it wasn't working and they'd have to go for other outfits. The band wore clothes that went well together but weren't identical.

Harry moved into the *X Factor* house with the other 15 acts the day after his audition was shown on TV, and because of this he started to be recognised. For him, the *X Factor* journey had started months ago, but for the general public it was only just beginning and they were still waiting to see whether he made it through bootcamp. Living in the house were three acts from each category, plus a wildcard. The property was a £3.5 million mansion near Borehamwood in north London and it was like nothing Harry had ever seen before. To get to it, the contestants had to go along a private road, and the *X Factor* production team had hired security guards to prevent any overexcited fans from trespassing. It was in a more rural location than the houses chosen in previous years because of the noise of fans screaming for the contestants to come out and meet them, day and night.

DID YOU KNOW?

Harry and the rest of One Direction loved the beanbag room in the *X Factor* house, which had an L-shaped couch, huge beanbags to sit on, a big TV, a table tennis table and a Wii. Harry also liked the music room, which had a jukebox and a piano for when they wanted to rehearse together or just chill out to some music.

During the week, when they were rehearsing, Harry would wear casual, comfortable clothing that still looked good but didn't restrict him. Because his mum wasn't there to help him, he had to wash and iron his own clothes in the house, as well as having to cook. Harry loved the OnePiece Norwegian jumpsuits they were given: his was white and it was like wearing a big babygro. He would zip the hood up and run around and no one could work out who he was, apart from the other members of One Direction because they had one too (Liam's was blue, Zayn's was green, Louis had grey and Niall's featured an American Stars and Stripes design).

One day, Harry was knocked over by overexcited fans on his way to the studio. He and the others had just got out of a car and were heading for the studio door when it happened. The fans didn't mean to do it; they were just really excited to see him. As soon as Harry fell, Liam shouted over to check that his bandmate was okay; he wanted to help him to his feet but he couldn't because there were so many fans crowded around him. Harry managed to stand up and made it to the studio, still smiling away as if nothing had happened. It was at moments like these that he must have thought how his life had changed – he was in school one minute and the next, he was being followed by hundreds of girls, all wanting his autograph!

On his first night in the house, Harry joined in a singsong with the other contestants. Matt Cardle played guitar and they all relaxed and got to know each other a bit better. Although they would be competing against each other once the live shows started, they were determined to be friends. As the weeks went by it would prove tougher, as Harry would have to say goodbye to some good friends, but at least he'd still have Niall, Zayn, Liam and Louis.

At their first ever press conference, Harry admitted to GMTV: 'The house is always pretty loud. You have your messy people and your tidy people, but it's really good living with all the boys. I miss my mum a little bit, though.'

Having to share a bedroom helped the boys to bond, but it

was difficult trying to fit in all their stuff. Louis told the backstage cameras: 'Living in the contestants' house, it's good to be in a group 'cos if we ever have any problems, or on the flip side, if we're up for a laugh, then I've got four other lads to turn to, so it's great.

'We all stay in the same room: it's pretty much what you'd expect from five teenage lads – it's an absolute tip most of the time!'

The boys and girls had separate bathrooms in the house, which meant that the girls kept theirs clean but the boys' had boxer shorts, clothes and empty drink cartons scattered about.

Harry and his fellow bandmates loved their newfound independence and had loads of fun. Liam summed up what living in the house was like to the *Shropshire Star*. 'It's different,' he said. 'If you don't get to see it and experience it first-hand, you wouldn't understand what it's like. It's so much fun. There is never a dull moment, and it is always loud in the house. That's usually probably coming from our band! Everyone has such a great time and it is surprising how well everybody gets on because at the end of the day, it is a competition, but everybody gets on great.'

As the weeks went on and acts started to leave the competition some bedrooms became available, so Liam and Zayn decided to move into their own room, leaving Harry, Niall and Louis in the original one. It made sense, because they were so cramped; they had accumulated more and more stuff as the weeks went by. Harry had even been given free clothes to wear by a Covent Garden store hoping for some exposure.

DID YOU KNOW?

Niall says his most annoying habit is that he farts a lot, but he thinks the fact that he doesn't snore is a good thing. He thinks Harry's worst habit is that he gets naked a lot.

Harry is happy in his own skin and he wasn't afraid to strip off and get naked while living in the *X Factor* house. Sometimes he even stripped off when the cameras were there. To Harry stripping off feels right, and he would often walk round his mum's house in his boxers (hopefully putting some clothes on when they had visitors!).

DID YOU KNOW?

When he was performing on *The X Factor* Harry liked to wear green boxer shorts and Louis chose American-themed ones with stars. Harry also likes Tommy Hilfiger boxers.

While living in the *X Factor* house Harry used to wear a snake-print gold thong, which freaked out some of the female contestants. He confessed to a journalist for the *Mirror* at the time: 'My favourite party trick is to wear nothing but a gold thong in the house. My friend bought it for me for my birthday. The Belle Amie girls say I prance around the house in it – I'd say it's more of a slow, gentle stroll...'

DID YOU KNOW?

When Harry was at school he used to pull his pants down to reveal his bum when people weren't expecting it because he found it really funny.

A few weeks after moving into the *X Factor* house, the One Direction boys had great fun filming 'Harry's naked problem' for the *Xtra Factor*. In the video Niall, Zayn, Liam and Louis sit around the kitchen table talking to the camera while Harry (completely naked) makes himself a bowl of cereal. 'I'm really, really worried about Harry,' Louis ''fesses'. 'I feel like he's going nuts. He just can't, he just can't keep his clothes on and it's interrupting our practices. How are we supposed to concentrate when he's walking around in the nude?' Liam agrees, saying, 'We just want to be singers, good singers, and we're trying to concentrate and he's getting naked every time. There's absolutely nothing we can do about it.' 'He's always in the nude!' Louis adds.

While Liam and Louis are talking to the camera, Harry moves around the kitchen, his privates hidden by various objects. They all had to be very coordinated to get it right – when he moved to the table, Zayn looks through an *X Factor* book and passes it to Niall at just the right time, so that Harry can move at the same time and be appropriately covered. The video ends with Harry grabbing the book and moving out of the camera's range. (It did take more than one take to get it right, though, as Harry and Zayn mistimed the book move once so that Harry revealed too much!)

In another episode of *Xtra Factor*, a short clip showed Harry in their bedroom, sitting up on the top bunk without any clothes on. An *Xtra Factor* logo had been added post-production.

Cheryl Cole, who was mentoring the Girls category that year, had never seen Harry naked, but she has seen more of him than most. When *Sugarscape* asked her whether she would date him, Cheryl replied, 'Harry? I've seen Harry in his boxer shorts… Harry's a little brother type, but I get it; the girls go crazy for him – and the women.'

Harry isn't the only member of One Direction to like stripping off. The group told the *Daily Star*: 'We have trouble keeping our clothes on. We've always got our kit off in the *X Factor* house – we love a bit of skin flashing.'

In an October 2011 interview with the *Sun*, Harry revealed

that he has four nipples, and since then the media have published any photos they can get of him without his top on. 'I've got four nipples,' Harry confessed to the paper. 'I think I must have been a twin, but then the other one went away and left its nipples behind!'

He also spoke of his love for getting naked, saying, 'Stripping off is very liberating – I feel so free. I think you could safely say I'm not shy.'

As well as being known for his love of taking his clothes off, Harry is known for his curly hair. His sister Gemma used to be his hairstylist but X Factor bosses banned her from cutting his hair as soon as he made it through to the live shows. Instead, he had to visit a backstage hairdressing room so that the stylists could do his hair before the live shows on Saturdays and Sundays. On the wall they put up a poster of Harry with hair stuck all over it and a 'Dirty Harry' headline was stuck on the mirror.

Adam Reed was the man in charge of making sure that Harry's hair looked good on The X Factor. Previously, he had worked with Lady Gaga and Madonna so Harry must have felt like a true star. Adam advised Harry that his hair's condition would improve if he only washed it once a week because the natural oils would start to flow. Occasionally he used dry shampoo on Harry's hair to get it looking its best.

As well as having his hair professionally styled Harry also had to get used to wearing makeup and having to moisturise his skin to keep it feeling soft and refreshed. The makeup artists on X Factor put gel on his eyebrows and balm on his lips. (After X Factor finished, Harry was to have a new hairstylist: Lou Teasdale.)

DID YOU KNOW?

In July 2012 a survey revealed that Harry's hairstyle was the most requested male hairstyle in Britain. Justin Bieber's look had been number one in 2011, but only managed to make number three in the 2012 list. David Beckham's hairstyle was number two, with TV presenter George Lamb in fourth and music producer Mark Ronson came fifth. Hairstylist Andrea Daley told the *Sun*, 'Harry's recognised what hair has done for Justin Bieber's career and wants his locks to help him be just as popular.'

When the band were appearing on *X Factor*, lots of One Direction's fans thought that Niall was a natural blond, but he isn't. He began dying his hair when he was 12 but started to get fed up with it once he'd been in One Direction for a while. Newspapers reported that he'd asked Simon whether he could dye it black but was told he couldn't. In July 2012 he posted a photo of himself without a top on and with what looked like purple hair dye on his head. It turned out to be just purple shampoo that his hairdresser had applied to get rid of the yellow tones in his hair but he fooled a few fans. Niall might not be dyeing his hair black right now but he might be in the future.

DID YOU KNOW?

Harry was voted the 21st Sexiest Man in the World in a poll by *Glamour* magazine. The winner was *Twilight*'s Robert Pattinson, who had taken the title four years in a row. Harry was the highest-ranking member of One Direction. Zayn was next at 27, followed by Niall at 34, Louis at 48 and Liam at 77.

CHAPTER 5

SINGING TO MILLIONS

Harry absolutely loved the *X Factor* live shows – he got to perform week in, week out onstage in front of millions of people with four of his closest friends. Every week there was tension when Dermot O'Leary announced who was safe and who was in the bottom two – but Harry and One Direction were sailing through. Every time 'One Direction' was called out they would give each other (and Simon) a massive hug.

ONE DIRECTIONS X FACTOR JOURNEY

Week one: Number 1s – 'Viva La Vida' by Coldplay

Week two: Heroes – 'My Life Would Suck Without You' by Kelly Clarkson

Week three: Guilty Pleasures – 'Nobody Knows' by Pink

Week four: Halloween – 'Total Eclipse of the Heart' by Bonnie Tyler

Week five: American Anthems – 'Kids in America' by
  Kim Wilde
Week six: Elton John – 'Something About the Way You
  Look Tonight'
Week seven: The Beatles – 'All You Need Is Love'
Week eight: Rock – 'Summer of '69' by Bryan Adams and
  'You Are So Beautiful' by Joe Cocker
Week nine: Semi-final – 'Only Girl in the World' by
  Rihanna and 'Chasing Cars' by Snow Patrol
Week ten: Final – 'Your Song' by Elton John, 'She's the
  One' by Robbie Williams and 'Torn' by Natalie Imbruglia

There were some ups and downs during the X Factor live
shows for Harry. In one week during the sound check he
went to sing but couldn't; he felt as if he was going to be
sick. He was taken to the doctors but it turned out he had
just had very bad stage fright. Poor Harry! The other boys
rallied round and he managed to control his nerves so that he
could perform on the Saturday night. He caught a bug
another week and was sick a few times, along with a few of
the other contestants.

Sinitta tweeted: 'Saw XF kids today, poor little Niall from 1
direction has a bad throat so was sent to doctor and Harry
threw up again, I think he may have a bug.

'Please put up some prayers for the wee ones, it's bad enough
without getting struck down, mind you Mary recovered in
time, I hope they will.'

Rebecca Ferguson (who would eventually come second in
the competition) had been ill that week, too, and revealed in an
interview for the official X Factor website: 'We're all dropping
like flies! Storm [a contestant] and Harry are seeking medical

advice so we're all really worried about them.' However, Harry and Niall did recover enough to perform that week, which must have been a relief for Louis, Zayn and Liam.

Out of the 10 weeks of live shows, Harry was ill the most, with stage fright, stomach bugs, food poisoning and throat problems. One week Niall confessed to the official *X Factor Magazine*: 'The other night we'd got some food in but Harry felt a bit sick. He ran into the toilet but I was doing a poo at the time. He's shouting at me, "Get out the way, get out the way!", but I can't move because I'm on the loo. He ends up being sick into the bath. It turned out he burst blood vessels in his neck and he had to go to the doctor. He'd got food poisoning.'

DID YOU KNOW?

If Harry was having a dinner party and could invite three people, dead or alive, he would pick Michael Jackson, Elvis Presley and Freddie Mercury.

Another down during the live shows for Harry was in week six – Elton John week – when Aiden Grimshaw received the lowest votes and was sent home. Harry and the One Direction boys were very upset and didn't feel he deserved to go.

DID YOU KNOW?

At bootcamp the judges and hosts had secretly written down who they thought was going to win the series. Louis Walsh had predicted that Aiden would win; Simon and Nicole thought that Gamu Nhengu would win (she didn't make the live shows), and Dermot said Matt Cardle would be the winner.

If Simon Cowell had to say who his favourite member of One

Direction is he would more than likely say that as a professional he tries not to have favourites. However, we can guess that that it might be Harry because he thinks he has a great personality and is very likeable. He liked him from his very first audition. Harry rates Simon, too, and is so grateful for everything he has done for him personally and for One Direction as a whole. When it was Simon's birthday during their time on *X Factor* the boys decided to send him a joke present, as Harry explained to the *Mirror*: 'For Simon Cowell's birthday we got him a birthday card and taped £2.50 into it. That's 50p from each of us – he can buy whatever he wants with it.'

Even though Simon liked Harry, during One Direction's time on the show he wouldn't give him his mobile number. 'We would not be trusted with his number because me and Louis once gave out Matt's number on a Twitter cam,' Harry revealed in an interview with *Hits Radio*. 'It was an accident, don't judge us. I don't think Simon would take it as well as Matt did.' [The Matt Harry is talking about is Matt Cardle, who went on to win *The X Factor*.]

DID YOU KNOW?

Eventually the band were given Simon's number – and decided to make prank calls to him. They put on different accents and talked about his trousers being high.

Even though Simon hadn't thought at bootcamp that they had the potential to win the whole competition, after seeing the boys perform so well in the judges' houses round and in the first few weeks of the live shows, Simon changed his mind. He knew that Harry, Liam, Louis, Zayn and Niall had the potential to be in *The X Factor* final. When Aiden left the show it was a 'wake-up call' for Simon because Aiden had been a strong contender, and it made him commit even more time and energy into making sure that One Direction got better each week so they could secure a place in the final.

Although Louis Walsh, Dannii Minogue and Cheryl Cole were mentoring the boys' rivals they still heaped praise on them each week. In week five, after One Direction had sung 'Kids in America', Louis Walsh said to them, 'What a brilliant way to end the show! Listen, everywhere I go there's hysteria, it's building on this band. You remind me a bit of Westlife, Take That, Boyzone... you could be the next big band. I loved everything about the performance.'

Cheryl Cole added, 'That absolutely cheered me up and brightened up my night, I thoroughly enjoyed that performance. You are great kids: I love chatting to you backstage, you are just good lads, nice lads. Great performance, good song choice.'

The next week Dannii Minogue couldn't get over how good they were at the Elton John classic 'Something About the Way You Look Tonight'. 'Guys, you are so consistent, it's scary!' she said in her feedback. 'That song could have been really boring, but it was great – that's what I would love to hear you sing at your concerts, which I'm sure you will be doing one day [crowd cheers].'

Simon Cowell then made an announcement, telling everyone watching how much confidence he had in Harry, Zayn, Liam, Louis and Niall. 'This is the first time in all the years of *X Factor* where I genuinely believe a group are going to win this competition,' he proclaimed. 'And you know what? I want to say this, what was so impressive, you've seen the girls and anything else, and you've remained focused; you've been really nice to the crew, you're nice to the fans and most importantly, everything that happened tonight from the choice of song to what you wore, it was all down to you. Guys, congratulations!'

DID YOU KNOW?

In week eight – Rock week – Simon didn't choose the song 'Summer of '69' for the boys to sing, Harry did! He picked it because it was the first song that he ever performed with his band, White Eskimo. It means a lot to him and he thought One Direction could do a great version. He also chose *The Lion King* song, 'Something About the Way You Look Tonight', for Elton John week (week six) because it's a song he really loves.

After sailing through the semi-final after nine long weeks (and 11 amazing performances) the boys made it to the final, along with Matt Cardle, Cher Lloyd and Rebecca Ferguson. Harry's whole family were ecstatic; they'd been to every live show to cheer him on and put up with butterflies in their stomachs every Sunday night while they waited to hear if One Direction were in the bottom two or whether they'd be staying in for another week. Gemma was so proud of Harry that she didn't want to take off the special wristband she was given each week, but she had to in the end because her arm was full of them! She kept the week one wristband on, though.

In the days leading up to the final they got to visit home, and for Harry that meant going back to Holmes Chapel. The head teacher of Hermitage Primary School, Helen Jarrold, was so excited she allowed all the pupils from the school to walk down in their class groups to the village so they could support Harry; the cameras filmed at the school as the children waved flags they had made. Afterwards, they put up photos on the school website and had them up on a flat screen in the school's entrance for any visitors or parents to see.

In the final they sang 'Your Song', 'She's the One' and 'Torn'.

Sadly for Harry and the rest of One Direction they didn't win the show but finished in third place. The boys were all gutted and although they didn't cry on stage they shed plenty of tears afterwards. They really thought they were going to be the *X Factor* winners for 2010, but it wasn't to be.

The band might have been gutted that they lost but they didn't have much time to think about what was going to happen next because Simon Cowell told them to meet him in his office – and offered them an amazing £2-million recording contract with Syco, his record label. The actual winner of *X Factor*, Matt Cardle, only got a £1-million contract – so to be offered a £2-million contract was awesome. They couldn't tell anyone but Anne must have guessed when she saw Harry beaming from ear to ear that night. If he hadn't got a record deal, he definitely wouldn't have been in the mood to party.

Harry and the boys got to go home for Christmas, but they had to move permanently to London. There was no way Harry was going to college to do his A-levels! The boys knew that 2011 was to be an amazing year for them and they were looking forward to going on *The X Factor Live Tour* to perform at major arenas in the UK and Ireland. Before they went on the tour the boys were flown out to Los Angeles to start working on their album. There was no time to waste because their fans couldn't wait to rush out and buy their music.

It was strange for Harry to go from freezing England to sunny America; he didn't need his coats and sweaters, that's for sure. The boys weren't recognised abroad so they could chill out by the hotel swimming pool or go shopping if they had some free time; they could do the things that would now have been impossible in London.

After less than a week of recording, they had to fly back home as there were some important tour rehearsals for the

X Factor Live Tour that they couldn't afford to miss. They would be performing for up to 20,000 people on some nights and the stage was massive, so they had a lot to learn in a relatively short space of time. The performances would be a lot more physical than their *X Factor* performances as they had to do some dance routines, which had to be learnt before the first night in Birmingham's LG Arena on 19 February. They would also be singing one song they hadn't performed before, 'Forever Young', as well as 'Only Girl', 'Chasing Cars', 'Kids in America' and 'My Life Would Suck Without You'.

On the opening night Louis told the audience, 'Can you believe, five months ago we didn't even know each other, so thank you for making this happen. Thank you.' To come onstage and see fans holding up One Direction banners was something our favourite boy band will never forget. The tour got really good reviews, with the *Telegraph* reviewer noting that, 'The main draw for the girl-dominated crowd were Cowell-mentored boy band One Direction. Hysterical screams greeted their every move. Hyperventilating ensued when they ran through the crowd. When cheekily cherubic heart-throb Harry Styles danced to the front, squeals reached fever pitch. The merchandise sellers knew their market – judging by their stalls, you'd think this was a One Direction concert.'

As soon as the tour dates had been announced many teachers, parents and pupils from Harry's old primary school had booked tickets. Mrs Jarrold wrote in her head teacher's blog on Saturday, 12 March 2011: 'What an evening we had at the MEN Arena watching the *X Factor* tour and of course One Direction. I know many of you went to the show in the afternoon and the evening one too. We all felt very proud and happy for Harry Styles!'

> **DID YOU KNOW?**
>
> All *The X Factor* finalists swapped numbers when they were on the show, but afterwards Harry and the One Direction boys had to change theirs so they lost contact with some of the acts.

> **DID YOU KNOW?**
>
> For Harry performing in Manchester was the tour highlight – lots of his family and friends were there to support him. He thought the loudest crowd was at the O2 in London or maybe Dublin. His favourite song to perform was 'Forever Young'.

There was a wrap party after the tour finished, which Harry found emotional. The performers had all spent so much time with each other that it was hard to say goodbye, even though they could keep in touch. Mary Byrne was going back to Ireland and other acts were dispersing across England. Some of them had managed to secure record deals so that was a big positive, but not everyone. The ones who hadn't been signed had to go back to their normal lives.

Harry and Louis decided to go skiing in Courchevel, France, together with two of their friends because it was the last time they'd be able to take a holiday for a while. Harry had never skied before so he had a lot to learn, but Louis taught him the basics.

A couple of fans who happened to be in the resort when the boys were there tweeted: '16/04/2011 proud to say I met @louis_tomlinson and @ harry_styles in a bowling alley in courchevel. I met you in courchevel. Best day of my life.'

The paparazzi didn't follow them there, which was a good

thing, but one photo of them waiting to go with their skis on and another of Harry, wearing bright orange ski trousers, with a fan on the slopes did circulate on Twitter.

DID YOU KNOW?
Orange is Harry's favourite colour.

Harry's sister Gemma initially only told her close friends at university that Harry was her brother because she didn't want people to treat her differently, but after One Direction finished third on *The X Factor* she couldn't keep it a secret any longer. Big fans of the boys recognised her on the street and started pointing and shouting, 'It's Gemma Styles' – she has more than 600,000 fans on Twitter now!

Gemma got to see Harry every week when he was on *The X Factor*, but once the show finished she didn't get to see him very much at all because he was busy touring and then recording for One Direction's first album. Whenever she can, she visits him but it is difficult because she lives in Sheffield. When she's on her university holidays she flies out to see him wherever he is and they also catch up using Skype, Twitter and their mobile phones the rest of the time.

DID YOU KNOW?
Once, after they'd been for a family meal at T.G.I. Friday's, Harry was sick all over Gemma because he'd eaten too much!

CHAPTER 6

UP ALL NIGHT

efore signing up for *The X Factor* Harry had never had singing lessons; he'd just sung with White Eskimo. Although Simon was impressed with his first audition he could tell that Harry needed some vocal training, as did all the boys if they were to reach the desired standard. Simon had hired Savan Kotecha to be the lead vocal coach on *X Factor* and he worked with Harry and the One Direction boys a lot because learning to sing as a group and harmonise is much harder than singing individually. Savan is one of the best vocal coaches in the world and he is a fantastic songwriter too, having written songs for Westlife, JLS, Britney Spears, Usher, Leona Lewis and many more international stars.

During an interview with *Digital Spy* in May 2011 Savan was asked whether he had enjoyed being a vocal coach on *X*

Factor. 'It was a bit intense!' he told them. 'More so than I thought it would be, but it was fun. It reignited my passion for music. I've been doing this since I was 17 years old and after you've been lucky enough to have a decent amount of hits and success, you almost end up a little jaded. You start thinking, "Why wasn't my song a single?", rather than thinking, "Oh my gosh I'm a songwriter!" So being around the kids, especially the younger ones reignited that – you're around people like you were when you were trying to make it. It brought those feelings back and reignited my spark.'

Savan and Harry are really close friends and love working together. Harry and the other One Direction boys learnt so much from working with him in their lessons during *X Factor*, and they had a lot of fun too. They created some great backstage videos with him, including one featuring a song that Savan had written called 'Vas Happenin' Boys'. In it he sings about Harry being a slob and needing to win the *X Factor* because he can't get a job and that his dad could be Mick Jagger. He also sings that Niall was raised by leprechauns, Louis needs a boat, Liam looks sad when he sings, and that Zayn is the master of echoes. It's a very funny song, so check it out on YouTube if you haven't seen it already.

Savan had to start with the basics when coaching Harry, Niall, Louis and Zayn, although Liam had had some vocal training before. He taught Harry how to sing from his diaphragm rather than his throat, which is something that all professional singers need to do. He got Harry to lie on the floor so he felt relaxed and then told him to breathe as if he was sleeping. Harry did as he was told and although it felt strange singing while lying down he noticed the difference straight away. In a backstage video Harry revealed, 'You can tell the difference when you stand up. I thought you were joking the first time you told me to lie on the floor, but I can see that it works now.' He was also taught how important it was to warm his voice up before going onstage. If he rushed his warm-ups or didn't bother with them, he risked permanent damage to his voice.

Harry didn't have to say goodbye to Savan after *The X Factor* finished because he was going to be one of their songwriters. On their first album alone he co-wrote 'What Makes You Beautiful', 'I Wish', 'One Thing', 'Na Na Na', 'Up All Night' and 'Save You Tonight'.

DID YOU KNOW?

After listening to a few seconds of the opening of 'What Makes You Beautiful' Harry and the boys knew it was perfect for them; they loved it and thought it would be a great first song. They had been looking for a feel-good summer song with a catchy tune.

Savan wasn't the only world-class songwriter that the boys got to work with on the first album. They also worked with the award-winning producer and songwriter Steve Robson, who has worked with Take That, Faith Hill, Leona Lewis, Olly Murs, James Martin and many more huge stars. He co-wrote 'Everything About You' and 'Same Mistakes' with Wayne Hector. Wayne has written over 30 number-one hits and has worked with Westlife, JLS, The Wanted, Pixie Lott and Nicki Minaj. Rami Yacoub was the producer behind Britney Spears' '…Baby One More Time' and has written and produced many of her biggest hits. He co-wrote 'What Makes You Beautiful', 'I Wish' and 'One Thing' with Savan and Carl Falk.

The band were also given the opportunity to work with producer RedOne, a legend in the music world. His real name is Nadir Khayat and he worked with Michael Jackson on his last ever album, *Invincible*, and has produced some of Lady Gaga's biggest hits. Zayn believes working with RedOne gave their first album, *Up All Night*, an anthemic quality. He told the *Daily Star*, 'To work with RedOne was such a big deal. It's more like the sound he created with Nicole Scherzinger. Powerful.'

Up All Night also included tracks written by Kelly Clarkson, Ed Sheeran and Tom Fletcher (of McFly fame). Sony were very excited to get the opportunity to work with One Direction, and Sonny Takhar, the chief executive officer of Syco Records, said in an interview with *Music Week*: 'We started working with the band immediately after the show had finished – they went to LA and recorded with RedOne. Then, while the boys were out on the *X Factor* tour between February and April, we started finding and sourcing songs and creating situations where songs were written for the boys in preparation for them to record once they had finished.'

Up All Night track list:
1. 'What Makes You Beautiful'
2. 'Gotta Be You'
3. 'One Thing'
4. 'More Than This'
5. 'Up All Night'
6. 'I Wish'
7. 'Tell Me a Lie'
8. 'Taken'
9. 'I Want'
10. 'Everything About You'
11. 'Save You Tonight'
12. 'Stole My Heart'

Limited edition – Yearbook
13. 'Stand Up'
14. 'Moments'

Before the album was released fans across the world could do 1DCyberpunk challenges (set up by the boys' publicity team). Liam explained during the *Up All Night* Listening Party: '1DCyberpunk is actually the person who stole our laptop, has hidden it for ages, we can't find it anywhere and she's had little challenges for everyone to do to get pictures and stuff of us, loads of different things, so it's been a lot of fun for everyone.'

Fans followed 1DCyberpunk on Twitter http://Twitter.com/1DCyberpunk or on Facebook www.Facebook.com/1DCyberpunk. One Direction tried to help as much as possible by hashtagging #SAVETHE1DAY.

Zayn joked: 'It's not really that fun for us because we've not been able to get on the internet.'

One of the challenges resulted in 100,000 paper dolls of Harry, Niall, Liam, Louis and Zayn being made. Another was called 'Trick or Tweet' and it was Niall's favourite; Liam and Zayn preferred '1DCyberbeauty'. For 1DCyberpunk herself the highlights were: seeing fans dress like her for Halloween, the #1DGottaBeStars challenge where fans did their own videos for '*Gotta Be You*', the #1DPAPERRACE challenge, the #1DDIRECTORY trending challenge, the #1DEVERYWHERE challenge, #1DGAMER– and having 50,000 followers on Twitter. Here's a list of challenges set by Cyberpunk:

Challenge 1, #1DSUPERFAN, Code: SUPERFAN,
  Result: Won

Challenge 2, #1DLOVESCALES, Code: DIGIHEART, Result: Won

Challenge 3, #1DDIRECTORY, Code: YUMYUM, Result: Won

Challenge 4, #1DPAPERRACE, Code: MYOWN1D, Result: Lost

Challenge 5, #1DEVERYWHERE, Code: B0YP1C, Result: Won

Challenge 6, #1DFASHION, Code: MAKEME, Result: Won

Challenge 7, #1DWEBMIXER, Code: BACKCHAT, Result: Won

Challenge 8, #1DWHEREISCYBERPUNK, Code: FANCLUBS, result: Won

Challenge 9, #1DCYBERBEAUTY, Code: PRETTY, Result: Won

Challenge 10, #1DTRICKORTWEET, Code: 1DAAAH, Result: Won

Challenge 11, #1DGOTTABEYOU, Code: Y0UW0N, Result: Won

Challenge 12, #1DGOTTABESTARS, Code: MASH3D, Result: Won

Challenge 13, #1DLINGO, Code: HUBBUB, Result: Won

Challenge 14, #1DGAMER, Code: 8UTT0N, Result: Won

Challenge 15, #1DPAPERCODE, Code: ONLYYOU, Result: Won

Challenge 16, #1DCYBERBIRTHDAY, Code: CPCAK3, Result: Won

Challenge 17, #1DXFACTOR, Code: GUITAR, Result: Won

The exclusive album listening party, hosted by singer Diana Vickers, was held shortly before *Up All Night* was due to be released and had Harry and the boys debuting some of their songs from the new album. At the party, Niall admitted that the track he finds hardest to sing on the album is 'What Makes You Beautiful' because he has to sing the top harmony. Liam finds 'Moments' difficult because he has to go high, and Louis finds 'Save You Tonight' tricky because the chorus is high. Zayn can't decide which is harder – 'Save You Tonight' or 'Tell Me A Lie'. Harry agrees with Niall and told Diana Vickers, 'I would say "What Makes You Beautiful" because it's like quite high, you don't get much breath, so I'd say that one.'

The first song they decided to play was 'Up All Night' because it's the name of the album, and for the second they picked 'Moments' as it's one of their favourite songs on the album. The two songs are very different, which allowed them to show the variety of tracks on the album. While the songs played the boys walked around the room and admired the hundreds of photos of fans making heart shapes with their hands that had been posted on the walls, the paper dolls, sketches they had done, and read some of the Twitter messages. The third song they picked was 'One Thing'.

DID YOU KNOW?

The cover photo for the album was taken in Camber Sands, East Sussex. The lads were just having fun on the beach and it was really windy. They didn't want a posed shot; they wanted it to be natural.

The fourth song they chose to debut was 'More Than This'. 'This is my favourite song on the album,' Harry explained. 'This is a deep one.' After just one second of the song playing Diana said a tweet from Cyberpunk had come in which said that their laptop had been found, but then she said it hadn't, and they were having a quick-fire round. Harry was asked,

'Ducks with shoes or cows with hats?', but he couldn't answer properly because it was a silly question. The others had been asked more sensible questions: Niall had been asked, 'Male directioners or female directioners?' (he picked female, obviously); Liam was asked, 'Eyes or smile?' (he chose eyes); Louis was asked, '"What Makes You Beautiful" or "Gotta Be You"?' (he went for 'Gotta Be You'); and Zayn was asked, 'X Factor or Britain's Got Talent?' (he picked X Factor).

It turned out that 'More Than This' had been cut off because of a technical glitch, so Harry explained that it was going to be played again. He really took charge of the situation and sorted it all out; he wanted the fans to hear his favourite song. After it had played, their final song at the listening party – 'I Want' – came on. Diana then said that a tweet had come in from Cyberpunk and that the location of the laptop was underneath the sofa they were sitting on. After they'd found it, they all jumped on Zayn!

One of the best weeks of Harry's life so far was when Up All Night was released in Ireland on 18 November and in the UK on 21 November 2011. He could walk into any music store and see a rack filled with his own album! Back then, he had no idea that it would become a huge hit worldwide when it was released in other countries in early 2012.

In the UK alone Up All Night sold 138,163 copies in its first week of release, making it number two in the charts behind Rihanna's Talk That Talk, which sold 163,819 copies. In America, the album did even better, taking the number one spot on the Billboard 200 chart after selling an incredible 176,000 copies in the first week of its release. One Direction was the first UK/Ireland group to do this with their debut album – Harry couldn't believe it. When he looks at the album cover, even now he can't believe that it's him and his four mates, it just doesn't sink in.

The first single One Direction released was 'What Makes You Beautiful' and it was the most pre-ordered single Sony Music had ever had; it went to number one on iTunes within 15 minutes of being released. In its first week of release in the UK on Sunday, 11 September 2011, the single topped the charts, knocking Maroon 5 down to number two with 'Moves Like Jagger'. Pixie Lott was number three with 'All About Tonight', The Saturdays were number four with 'All Fired Up' and Olly Murs was at number five with 'Heart Skips a Beat'.

'What makes You Beautiful' was One Direction's first proper music video as a band. They had filmed a charity single video with the other *X Factor* acts but this was different. For a start, it was filmed at a beach in Malibu, California. In the video the boys ride around in an orange camper van, with Louis driving. He was very nervous, so drove slowly – which resulted in them twice getting pulled over by the US cops.

The director was John Urbano, who has directed music videos for Lissie and Alexi Murdoch. Filmed over two days in July 2011, the boys' video was released on 19 August 2011. The story of the video is that One Direction are meeting up with three female friends and going to the beach, and that Harry is in love with one of the girls, who doesn't know she's beautiful. They have fun on the beach and then relax around a campfire. The actress chosen to play the girl was called Madison and Louis liked to joke that Harry had fallen for her. One Direction shot these scenes on the first day and then on the second day they shot scenes at a different location. While they were filming Louis thought it was a good idea to jump off a ledge high up into the sand, so Liam did it too. It was a bit risky because they could have hurt themselves.

The director loved working with them and told the backstage cameras: 'The video's been going great; it's been a ton of fun. Working with the guys... they're amazing, they work so well with each other, you know – it's like they've been best friends for ever and that's exactly what we're looking for.' When they'd finished the shoot the boys all celebrated by going for a swim in the sea.

DID YOU KNOW?

When Harry was doing a bit of sunbathing on the beach he fell asleep, so Zayn decided to cover him with sand. He got a shock when he woke up with just his head sand-free!

DID YOU KNOW?

Harry once said: 'I wish I had a girl to cuddle up to at night rather than my pillow.'

'What Makes You Beautiful' was released in America in February 2012 and reached number four in the charts. Singer/songwriter Katy Perry was chuffed for the boys, tweeting to Niall: 'Congratulations, you didn't let me down! Xo'. He replied: 'Let's hope it holds out this week! Thank you for putting me thru! We've been working hard, I won't let you down.' (Katy had been one of the judges during the first Irish auditions in Dublin.)

Girls around the world fell in love with the song, and with One Direction. 'What Makes You Beautiful' was number one in Ireland and Mexico, number two in New Zealand, number three in Japan, number seven in Australia and Canada, to name just a few. To date it has sold over five million copies worldwide. Liam said the boys felt humbled to have the song do so well, telling BBC Radio 1, 'We have an incredible team of people around us who have helped us achieve this. Above all we would like to thank our fans. We owe all our success to them.'

One Direction's second single to be released was 'Gotta Be You', with the video once again shot by John Urbano. This time it was filmed at the State University of New York at Plattsburgh and at Lake Placid, New York. They filmed in October 2011 and fans got to see it for the first time on 8 November 2011. In the video the boys are students, leaving school and making their way to the lake to have a bonfire with some female friends. Niall gets to play his guitar, which was significant for him because he loves playing it. Louis drives a Mini Cooper, Zayn takes the train, Liam travels in a blue Beetle car and Harry goes on a red scooter. The video finishes with a firework display and a silhouette of Zayn walking towards a girl and kissing her.

'Gotta Be You' was released on 11 November 2011 and did well in the charts considering that the boys didn't do that much promotion. It was number three in the UK and Ireland, behind Rihanna's 'We Found Love' and Flo Rida's 'Good Feeling'. The girl in the video was an American model called Emma Ostilly and Harry posted a photo of the two of them on Twitter. When One Direction were in New Zealand, Emma was there and the press got hold of a photo of them kissing in the early hours of the morning after Harry had dropped her off at the place where she was staying. Following this, Emma received so many nasty messages that she temporarily closed down her Twitter account.

One Direction's third single in the UK and Ireland was 'One Thing'; it was their second release in other countries. The boys had a great time filming the video in London on 28 November, with Louis explaining to Real Radio:

'Basically, there wasn't much of a script for the video... it was more like, we're going to go to these different locations, be yourself, do what you want to do and for me it's our, probably, most real and more like us video that we've had so far... it worked really well.' They invited fans to be in the scenes at Trafalgar Square and thanked them afterwards. Harry tweeted: 'Big thanks to everyone who got involved in our video yesterday!

'It was fun, and hopefully you'll like it. Video 3... done!'

In an interview with Capital FM he said, 'It was amazing! It was literally us being idiots around London for a day and we filmed it.'

'One Thing' was released in the UK on 13 February 2012 – the day before Valentine's Day. It was released on 22 May 2012 in the US and available for digital download on 6 January 2012 in Austria, Denmark, Estonia, France, Germany, Greece, Hungary, Italy, Latvia, New Zealand, Poland, Portugal, Spain and Switzerland. In the UK it charted at number nine in the UK, 39 in the US, number three in Australia, number four in Hungary and number six in Ireland. The B-side to the single was 'I Should Have Kissed You'.

'One Thing' only just made it onto the album, as Niall explained on the *Ralphie Radio Show*: 'We actually had nearly finished the album and "One Thing" was one of the last songs we recorded. We actually flew to Sweden just to do "One Thing" and "I Wish" 'cos we felt this was a cracking song and we needed to record it so it was actually one of the last songs... it's like the perfect like "cousin" to "What Makes You Beautiful". It's the same kinda vibe, really punchy chorus, so you know we just wanted to make another good song.'

> ## DID YOU KNOW?
> There is a great spoof of the video on YouTube, with five babies playing Niall, Harry, Liam, Louis and Zayn. To check it out, just search for 'One Direction One Thing Babies' on YouTube. Harry really likes it and tweeted: 'I really want to meet these guys!!' to which Niall replied: '@Harry_Styles no harry you want to meet their mums'. It has been viewed over two million times. The babies have done other One Direction videos and have their own blog: http://mill1122112.blogspot.co.uk/

When they visited Sweden in the February 2012 Niall had tweeted: 'Sweden you legends! Mad day in Stockholm! All the interviews n stuff! And directioners everywhere! #1Dinsweden' – and it was soon trending worldwide.

In a tweet Niall wrote on 18 June 2012 he said: 'Been to so many countries now! Sweden, Germany, France, Italy, Holland, Australia, New Zealand, Mexico, US, Canada, loving this journey, its [sic] been sick.' Every new place they visited offered the chance to meet and thank fans for their support. Shortly before they visited Mexico for the first time, Niall tweeted: 'Our first time in South America! Mexico here we come! Cannot wait, ive heard audiences down there are crazy! #1DinMexico #vivamexico'.

Their fourth and final release from *Up All Night* was 'More Than This'. For this single the boys didn't film a special music video; the video was just footage from their tour of the band performing the song. It was released first in Australia for digital download on 25 May 2012 and later released in the UK and USA on 26 June 2012. It reached number 49 in the Australian charts, number 86 in the UK, and number 39 in Ireland.

DID YOU KNOW?

According to Amazon, One Direction's 2012 Calendar was the top-selling calendar ever.

The Amazon top 10 bestselling calendar list:
1. One Direction 2012 Calendar
2. Cheryl Cole 2011 Calendar
3. JLS 2011 Calendar
4. Cliff Richard 2011 Calendar
5. JLS 2010 Calendar
6. Take That 2010 Calendar
7. Take That 2011 Calendar
8. Justin Bieber 2011 Calendar
9. Cliff Richard 2010 Calendar
10. JLS 2012 Calendar

Although their song 'Tell Me A Lie' was never released as a single, the One Direction boys really liked it. It was written by Kelly Clarkson, who originally planned to include it on her 2011 album, S*tronger*, but was more than happy to let Harry and the boys have it. 'It's a really cute song – I love it,' Kelly gushed to Ryan Love from *Digital Spy* before the album was released. 'I loved that they liked it. They sound really great on it. I already have it – I'm so VIP with my copy on my computer! It does sound really good.'

The deluxe edition of the album included the pop ballad 'Moments' and 'Stand Up'. Fans with the deluxe edition also got a hardback yearbook with lots of photos, lyrics, drawings and quotes from the One Direction boys. 'Moments' was written by singer/songwriter Ed Sheeran when he was 15 and he even thought then that it was a boy-band song. It is Louis' favourite track from the album.

DID YOU KNOW?

Ed has 100 songs on his iPod that he has written for other bands/artists to sing. Niall likes to listen to James Morrison, Olly Murs and Jessie J on his iPod. His most played song is 'You Give Love a Bad Name' by Bon Jovi. Harry loves listening to *Noel Gallagher's High Flying Birds* album, but the others like to joke that one of the most played tracks on his iPod is 'Reach for the Stars' by S Club 7. Harry denies this is true but does admit that the most embarrassing song on his iPod is the 90s track 'Saturday Night' by Whigfield!

CHAPTER 7

FINDING HOME

After *X Factor* finished Harry and the boys moved out of the *X Factor* house into a hotel and then into an apartment, paid for by their record company. They all lived together but after a while Harry and Louis decided to get their own place, because they are such good friends and it was a bit cramped with the five of them sharing.

Harry's mum revealed what her son's bedroom in London is like, telling a reporter from the *People*, 'In Harry's bedroom there are clothes everywhere, posters from clothes shops, trendy things from catalogues.

'He has a brown and cream colour scheme but the clothes are everywhere. He's pretty messy, it is his worst habit.'

The apartment that Harry and Louis decided to rent in Princess Park Manor, Friern Barnet, north London is extremely luxurious. If they had chosen to buy instead of rent it would have cost them £3 million. Cheryl and Ashley Cole used to live there when they were dating – the rent is currently £5,000 a month!

A source told the *Daily Star*: 'Harry and Louis are living the life of luxury and loving every single minute... they had a wild bash with Louis hiring a coach to bring his old school chums. Harry was telling everyone he's fallen head over heels for the flat, and loved the fact Ashley Cole used to live there.

'Most lads dream of lording around a footballer's pad, so Harry and Louis have earned bragging rights.'

The flat is in a building that used to be the Colney Hatch Lunatic Asylum in Victorian times and the other One Direction boys lived in a flat in the same complex so they were always coming round. They were surrounded by 20 acres of parkland, so it was peaceful. The boys didn't end up staying in the flat for long because of the touring they had to do, but Harry's fans were still interested in seeing what it looked like after photos were shown on the internet when the company who manage it were looking for a new tenant.

The apartment is called 'The Dome' and has five floors. It has a 360-degree kitchen, three luxury bedrooms with ensuites, living room, a top floor cinema room, and even has its own lift. The complex has its own gym, private minibus and security gates.

Harry and Louis used to think it was funny when some fans gave them the nickname 'Larry' because they are so close and joked that they were an item, but now they are fed up with it. Louis in particular would like people to stop because he is in a serious relationship. 'This is a subject that was funny at first but now is actually hard to deal with, as I am in a relationship,' he told *Storyboard*. 'Me and Harry are best friends. People look into our every move – it is actually affecting the way me and Harry are in public.

'We want to joke around, but there seems to be a different rumour every time we do anything; I act the same way with Harry as I do with any of the other boys.'

The press seem to enjoy giving a Harry a hard time about his love life and there are lots of internet 'trolls' who write nasty things about Harry and his family too. Zayn hates seeing people being so mean to him and told the *Sun*, 'He is the baby of the group but people seem to forget that because of the way that he is and that he is so charming.

'It does annoy us a bit. He's a young kid and people are just giving him grief for no reason.'

In June 2012 Harry started looking to buy his own place, viewing properties in Primrose Hill, northwest London. Louis was in America, so Harry took along the One Direction hairstylist and makeup artist Lou Teasdale as she is now a good friend and he trusts her judgement. Photos of them together were soon circulating on the internet and Twitter as if they were dating – it was all a bit silly as Lou is in a committed relationship and has a young daughter.

You should check out Lou's fashion blog (http://louteasdale.tumblr.com/) and her daughter's Twitter account (https://Twitter.com/Real_BabyLux). The boys adore Lux and love spending time with her and giving her presents. On her Twitter page you can see lots of photos of her with Harry and the others that you won't see anywhere else. Harry tweeted a photo of Lux with a toy giraffe and it trended worldwide in May 2012. When the boys went to London Fashion Week in September 2012, Lou posted a photo of Zayn and Louis in the front row, sporting quiffs, and wrote: 'Well

done lads xxx ps think it was coza ya hair :) #leo #dannyzuko'.
Her Twitter account is http://Twitter.com/louteasdale.

Niall loves Lou cutting his hair and in June 2012 he tweeted
a photo of her cutting someone else's hair, with him (wearing
no top) standing next to her with his arm around her. He
explained: 'Yess! @louteasdale is back! Got a hair cut'. Harry
had previously tweeted a photo of Lou cutting Niall's hair in
April, with Niall once again topless but trying to eat a plateful
of food at the same time.

After Harry bought his first home, he must have been
chuffed, and he soon had a neighbour he recognised: Zayn. His
One Direction bandmate decided to buy a house nearby.
Harry's house is rumoured to have cost him £3 million; it has
four bedrooms, three reception rooms and three bathrooms. It
has a double car lift and a big garden and is in an exclusive part
of north London.

DID YOU KNOW?

Even though Harry lives in London now, Holmes Chapel
will always be home to him. Some people that were at
school when Harry was, and others he has never met but
who live in Holmes Chapel, have been abusive towards
Harry when he goes home to see his family. They swear
at him in the street and hurl abuse, and Harry doesn't
understand why. He never flaunts his success. His friend
Will spoke to *New!* magazine about it, saying, 'It really
upsets Harry because he's a sensitive guy,' adding, 'More
recently he's had abuse on network sites and chat rooms.'

CHAPTER 8

RIVALRY

Apart from the contestants, every week on the *X Factor* Sunday night results show various singers and groups would perform their latest tracks. Harry and the rest of the contestants felt so privileged to be able to meet huge artists like Usher, Katy Perry, Michael Bublé, Rihanna, Bon Jovi, Kylie Minogue, Justin Bieber and The Black Eyed Peas. They also got to see other groups – JLS, The Wanted, Westlife and Take That all appeared on the show and Harry had the opportunity to chat to them afterwards. He could ask them what it was really like to be in a boy band long term and any other burning questions he might have had.

The press tried to say that there was a rivalry between One Direction and The Wanted when the boys were on the show and at the time both bands said there was room for them both so they wished each other well. In an interview with Heart FM in October 2010, Jay McGuiness from The Wanted said, 'When we arrived, JLS were really gracious and encouraged us to do well and work hard. I think if we did anything less, it would be a bit unfair, so I just wish them good luck because they're just trying to do what we're trying to do.'

Max George added, 'I really like them, actually – I think they're one of my favourites on there because they're the whole package.'

Since then both bands have had a bit of banter. When Chris Moyles from Radio 1 suggested that One Direction were more popular, Tom from The Wanted said, 'Our new single "I Found You" is a bit different. We like to mix it up – we try not to be stereotypical.'

Harry can't have been happy with this comment because he tweeted: 'Chris Moyles is actually right though. If 1D aren't [sic] in the picture, The Wanted would've been WAY more popular!'

In an interview that The Wanted did in September 2012, the interviewer wrongly thought that they were One Direction but instead of correcting the mistake, The Wanted lads went along with it for a laugh. During the interview Tom said, 'The Wanted are the coolest band in the world.' Max added, 'I've actually met them – they're really, really cool.'

In an April 2012 interview with *TMZ* it was suggested that One Direction might be intimidated by The Wanted but Nathan was quick to point out this wasn't the case. 'I think we intimidate a lot of people,' he said, 'but I am pretty sure we don't intimidate other teenage boys... it's all good. I was texting Liam earlier.'

Despite a bit of friendly banter, Harry and the One Direction boys would be willing to work with The Wanted on a charity single if the opportunity ever arose.

One of Harry's favourite moments from *The X Factor* was meeting Gary Barlow, Robbie Williams, Mark Owen, Howard Donald and Jason Orange from Take That. They are his favourite group, so meeting them was a dream come true. Gary is now an *X Factor* judge and had he been a judge in Series 7, Harry might have wanted him as his mentor!

The rest of One Direction also loved meeting Take That while they were on *The X Factor* (and at different awards shows and events since) but, apart from Louis, they like different groups more. Niall loves Westlife 'because they're Irish' and Liam and Zayn think 'N Sync were 'the best boy band ever!'

One Direction impressed Westlife when they met them for the first time in 2010. Shane Filan from Westlife told *X Magazine* at the time: 'They're the whole package: they're good singers, they're good-looking lads and they're quite cool. They're like a band full of Justin Biebers and they've got everything the girls will love.'

CHAPTER 9

GIRLS

Harry has always been popular with girls, even when he was really young. When he was nine years old he went on a family holiday to Cyprus and when it was time for him to go home some teenage girls that he had met there decided to wave him off when the coach came to pick him up. His dad remembers that holiday well and told the *Daily Record*: 'It's not just his looks but he's very charming, it's like a gift really. I always knew he'd succeed at whatever he did because he'd always charm people; from performing in the car or on holiday he'd always be able to hold a crowd or hold a room even when he was a kid.

'His sister has always been academically brilliant and when he was about 14 he would say, "I'll never live up to Gemma", but the tables are turned now through what's happened to Harry.'

Harry was 11 when he had his first kiss, and he had a few girlfriends while he was living in Holmes Chapel. He was, however, single when he auditioned for *The X Factor* and ever since then people have been constantly trying to set him up or suggest that he's dating girls that he's only just met. It's true that Harry is a bit of a flirt and likes having fun. He doesn't take himself too seriously and when asked to film a short clip for the *Xtra Factor* at bootcamp he jumped at the chance. In the clip, Konnie Huq, the *Xtra Factor* host, has noticed that Harry is flirting with a lot of the girls, so decides to set him up on a date. She lays out a table, some dinner and drinks and invites Harry to come along for a date with Katie, one of the other contestants who has a bit of a crush on him. Harry presents Katie with a rose and the two of them laugh together, acting as if they are getting on really well. However, when Katie has to go because she has been called onstage to perform, Harry starts chatting to another girl... and then a group of girls comes over and it's revealed that Harry has been flirting with them all. The clip ends when Wagner (one of the male contestants) comes in and carries Harry off!

During his time in the *X Factor* house, the press suggested that he was dating fellow contestant Cher Lloyd, but they were just friends. He told the *Mirror* at the time, 'We're friends with all the girls in the house. I bought Cher a pork pie, but she hasn't eaten it yet – it's still in the fridge.'

Harry loved it when girl group The Saturdays came to one of the *X Factor* Live Shows because his dream woman at the time was Frankie Sandford. He got to chat to her afterwards on the *Xtra Factor* but seemed quite overwhelmed and wasn't his normal flirty self. When interviewed later he revealed that he really likes girls with short hair like Frankie's.

> **DID YOU KNOW?**
> When Frankie found out that Harry had a crush on her, she said she thought the five years between them was too big an age gap, but that she likes his hair. She would rather look after One Direction than date one of them.

> **DID YOU KNOW?**
> Harry's mum Anne is 10 years younger than his dad, so she doesn't think age gaps are that big a deal.

If you fancy Harry you might want to know what he looks for in a girl. Harry likes girls who have cute faces and who are honest about how they feel. 'I think if you like someone, then you like that person – you shouldn't play games. You should ask them out,' he told *Tiger Beat*. And if you ever manage to meet Harry face-to-face and wanted to ask him out, he says, 'Walk up to me and just make conversation. I like someone who's easy to talk to!'

One clever fan saw Harry outside a branch of Subway and came up with the idea of trying to put her iPhone in his pocket. She got caught but Liam thought her approach was very clever because if she had succeeded, then Harry would've had to meet up with her to return the phone.

During their time on *The X Factor* one newspaper ran a story claiming that Liam had banned Harry, Zayn and Niall from dating during *The X Factor* (Louis was already dating someone). There was no truth in the story at all and a bemused Louis explained to *X Magazine*, 'Absolute tosh, the entire thing! Liam wouldn't be able to slap a girl ban on us if he tried.'

Liam continued, 'This is the first I've heard of it. Am I

supposed to have slapped a girl ban on myself, too? That would just be stupid.'

In August 2011, Harry admitted that One Direction like girls with banter and that he had a bit of a crush on *Xtra Factor* host Caroline Flack. In an interview for the *X Factor* website he said: 'Obviously, we like a girl to be attractive, but it's all about the banter – standard! And I like a babe with a talent – you need to be good at something. Like tennis! Now, that's cool.

'And if Caroline Flack is reading this, say "Hi" from me. She is gorgeous!'

In the same interview, Zayn admitted that his celebrity crushes are Megan Fox and Jessica Alba, and Niall said his were soap star Brooke Vincent (Sophie Webster in *Coronation Street*) and Pippa Middleton.

DID YOU KNOW?

Harry doesn't find it attractive when girls swear.

When rumours started circulating that Harry was dating Caroline Flack in November 2011, everyone wanted to know what his family thought – whether they felt really angry with Caroline because she was 32 and Harry was only 17. His sister Gemma set the record straight in an interview with *Heat* magazine. 'If he's happy, we're happy,' she said. 'We're always going to be supportive of each other, whatever happens in our lives. I guess we're quite liberal in that way. Harry's very thoughtful and caring: if he likes someone, he'll tell them. He won't hide how he's feeling.'

She also revealed that although Harry had dated girls in the past they had been 'teenage relationships' and he had never been in love.

The press reported that Harry took Caroline to meet his

family in January 2012 and they had dinner together. They also tried to suggest that they were very serious about each other and that they were in love, but Harry and Caroline didn't comment on it at all.

By late January it was all over, with the press claiming that Harry had dumped Caroline. He used Twitter to set the record straight, tweeting: 'Please know I didn't "dump" Caroline. This was a mutual decision. She is one of the kindest, sweetest people I know. Please respect that.'

Caroline had received nasty tweets and online abuse while they were together, and even when their relationship finished she still received some – along with comedians poking fun at her for dating someone so young. Seven months after they split she told *Look* magazine she was still getting stick and she was surprised at how negative people were. If she could turn the clock back she wouldn't delete Harry from her life, she said, adding, 'With the whole Harry situation, about 95 per cent of what was written was false. I didn't really know where to begin.

'But I've developed thicker skin and become more hardened to it. I don't get as upset as I used to, but I'm still human.'

In a separate interview with the *Mail on Sunday* she openly revealed that they were still mates. 'We remain very fond of each other because first and foremost we are friends,' she said. 'We got very close for a time but that's between me and Harry; what happened is between me and him, and then, you know, we decided it was best to be just friends.

'Harry is adorable, he is a nice person. He was nice to me; we were nice to each other. We are still friends, he's brilliant, he is so much fun.'

One of the things that hurt Caroline the most was an article published in an unofficial One Direction magazine, which was a full page of insults aimed at her. It portrayed her as a voodoo doll with 'crow's feet' and nicknamed her 'grandma'. It was truly awful and no true One Direction fan would write such cruel things. Caroline also had to move from her apartment in Camden because the paparazzi continually stalked her and she needed to feel safe in her own home again. She confided to *Fabulous* magazine, 'At my old place, the front door opened straight on to the street. And when you walk out and you've got 20 men staring at you with cameras it was embarrassing. I'd see my neighbours and say, "I'm so, so sorry".'

Since her relationship with Harry ended, people have tried to get her to date her *Xtra Factor* co-host Olly Murs, but that isn't going to happen (even though her mum would like it). She just sees him as a friend.

Harry's friend Will couldn't help but ask him about Caroline when they caught up with each other. Will told the *People*, 'All his mates think he's a bit of a legend, though. It's classic Styles. He definitely enjoys the attention and he's making the most of it.'

In April 2012, a single Harry admitted on *The Kyle and Jackie O Show* in Sydney that he is looking for 'someone who is fun, someone funny, someone you can have a conversation with'. He was staying in the same hotel as Rihanna, who is a fan of Harry and One Direction. She told the *Mirror:* 'Harry, yeah. I watch their videos and I remember thinking, "Wow, he's a star"… he seems very sure. It seems, like, it's so natural to him.'

In other interviews Harry has said that he likes women who play hard to get. He likes to flirt and told *Top of the Pops* magazine, 'The fun part is the chase, so if you speak to me, play a bit hard to get. I think it's attractive when someone turns you down. You don't want someone to say yes straight away, do you?'

His dad Des gave an interview to the *People* in June 2012 and revealed, 'There was a short period when he had several different girlfriends, one after the other, and I said, "Look, don't get a reputation because at some point the girls will catch on to that."

'He said "Yeah" and took it on board. But whether he tries to live by that mantra I've no idea. As far as I know Harry doesn't have a girlfriend at the moment.'

DID YOU KNOW?

Harry has only ever had one fight, and that was when he was in primary school, but he told *HollywoodLife*, 'I don't mind getting a black eye or a broken arm for a girl as long as she's there to kiss it after.'

A month later Liam also commented on Harry's single status and revealed that it was Harry who helped him find love with dancer Danielle Peazer (they have since split). Liam told i93 Dallas radio: 'This has never been told before, but when I actually got with my girlfriend Harry was the boy that set us up.

'Also, Louis and Eleanor as well, was also Harry. Harry's the magic match-up man. He's like Hitch, he can do it for everyone else... he's a lonely old man.'

Any girl who is lucky enough to date Harry or one of the other boys would be treated like a princess as they are all quite romantic. To show his loving side Harry says he would write a song for a girl and Liam says he would whisk his girl away on a romantic holiday. Their top three romantic songs are: 'I Don't Wanna Miss a Thing' by Aerosmith, 'Make You Feel My Love' by Adele and Lemar's 'The Way Love Goes'.

Harry admitted to *We Love Pop* magazine: 'I like girls, but I prefer having a girlfriend. I like having someone I can spoil, somebody to call up in the middle of the night and just talk to. I like getting close to someone like that.'

For Valentine's Day 2012 the boys were busy promoting 'One Thing' in France so they spent the day and night together, going out for a meal in a restaurant in Paris. It wasn't at all romantic but Harry did tweet fans to say: 'Happy Valentine's Day!!! We couldn't do this if it wasn't for you and we love you for that. Hope everyone has a lovely day! Oui Oui!!. X'.'

Niall tweeted: 'happy valentines day everyone, love you all so much if it wasn't for you there would be no 1D.'

(Niall did try to say 'bonjour' to the French fans that they met; he's quite good at speaking French after learning it at school and French interviewers are often impressed. He had never been to France before so he was very excited about the whole trip.)

DID YOU KNOW?

Directioners thought that the 'One Thing' video was 'amazayn' (it's the One Direction way of saying amazing!).

Any potential girlfriend of Harry's would have to impress his mum Anne because she means the world to him. You can tell they are super close from an interview Anne did with *Heat* magazine: 'He gives the best hugs ever. I love hugging him and kissing him when he comes home. He's a very caring and lovely guy – being in the group is the best thing that could have happened to him, because Harry wouldn't enjoy being out on the road on his own.'

DID YOU KNOW?

Harry might have kissed fans before. In an interview with *We Love Pop* magazine he was asked how many fans he had kissed. He replied: 'Maybe two... maybe...'

In the same interview he added: 'I got someone's number at a signing.

'I'd stayed at my friend's house for a couple of days and his local pub was round the corner, so I went in there with him and apparently she was behind the bar. At the signing she told me she'd seen me at the pub and gave me her number on the way out. I didn't even have to do anything!'

Anne thinks he will make a good boyfriend for someone when he's ready to settle down because he is sensitive and caring. 'He had one or two girlfriends when he was younger, but no one very special,' she revealed. 'I'd love Harry to have a family one day, and he'd love one, too. He'd make a fantastic dad.'

Anne is the most important woman in Harry's life, and always will be. She is the most popular One Direction mum and is determined to use her 'celebrity' status to raise as much money as possible for charity. In September 2012 she climbed Mount Kilimanjaro in Kenya with her friend Vicky Sherlock (who happens to be the mum of Harry's close friend Ashley). They took the difficult Machame route over 10 gruelling days.

She did the climb for the 'Believe in Magic' charity, which helps to make seriously and terminally ill children smile in the UK. The charity throws magical parties and gives the youngsters once-in-a-lifetime experiences. Harry encouraged One Direction fans to donate to her worthy cause, tweeting:

'Hi guys, my mum is climbing mount Kilimanjaro for charity and she goes tomorrow. You can sponsor her here if you want! http://t.co/10A2BsfP'.

Anne and Vicky wanted to raise £10,000 but before they had even caught the flight to Kenya they had raised over £20,000 on their sponsor page (www.justgiving.com/anne-vicky-webelieveinmagic). Anne explained on their page: 'We have been inspired by the founder of the charity, Meg, a very brave 16-year-old who is herself extremely poorly. This, however, doesn't stop her from working tirelessly to help other sick and terminally ill children to realise their dreams. By sponsoring us for our climb, you will be helping Meg to help the children who are referred to her have an experience they've dreamed about and give them something to look forward to!'

She went on to explain what the charity would like to do with the money: 'Believe in Magic would like to buy a holiday home where the children, along with their families, can have a break from their everyday lives and enjoy a change of scene. Small things like this we often take for granted... these children take nothing for granted.'

In a post dated Sunday, 19 February, she wrote: 'Myself and Vicky were privileged to be invited to attend the "Believe in Magic" Party at Hamleys and to meet some of the children and their families that are helped by the charity. These children are suffering the most dreadful illnesses, with such amazing courage and bravery and in many cases, very little hope of a happy ending. Their families are truly amazing. They are strong... so strong. They are all incredible and I know that the thought of these brave children and their families is what will help us on our trek up Mount Kilimanjaro.'

Harry's stepdad Robin didn't go on the trip with Anne

but he helped her raise money before she went. He had his chest waxed to encourage people to donate – and raised much more than he expected. The 'event' took place at the Antrobus Arms and Harry was there among the crowd. If you search on YouTube for 'Robin's Chest Waxing for Believe in Magic July 2012' you can see a video from the night that Anne has posted (Harry can be seen at 1 minute 18 seconds).

Anne wrote underneath the video: 'Robin (@robintwist) was very brave on Saturday night and had his chest waxed (or at least partially!) to raise money for Believe in Magic. The event was videoed and this is a little bit of evidence of how it went. The waxing raised in excess of £2000 so thank you Robin for putting yourself through it and thank you to all you generous/sadistic folk who paid for the privilege (and to Harry who paid for me to pull off a strip! ooohh)'.

DID YOU KNOW?

The press sometimes say that Anne and Robin are man and wife but they aren't yet – they are engaged. Harry's dad Des clarified things on Twitter in May 2012: 'Much "wrong" info re Harry on web. Not in LA to do solo deals, 1D rock solid, Mum not remarried to my knowledge, where do they get it from?'

In an interview with Radio 1 Anne was asked to grade Harry on different things. For texting her she gave him an A+, for calling her to say 'hello' she gave him a B+, for his ability to cook his family a meal she gave him an A-, for remembering her birthday she gave him an A★ because he's never forgotten. She also gave him a B- for making his bed when he comes home!

Harry likes to treat his mum to nice things so when he came back from America one time he gave her some shoes, although he doesn't get her a present every time he goes to a new place. The biggest present he has ever bought her was a new house! He gave her the keys on her birthday in 2012 to thank her for being such a great mum. The new home offers her more privacy than her old house.

DID YOU KNOW?

Harry is a good cook, and according to Anne he always has been. One of his favourite things to make is tacos. When he was younger he used to paint on bread with food colouring before toasting it.

When it was Anne's birthday on 21 October 2011 Harry asked fans to help make #happybirthdayanne trend on Twitter. Harry's stepdad Robin tweeted: '@anne42cox is giving it large in the wine bar #happybirthdayanne'.

Some One Direction fans have even set up fan pages for Anne on Facebook and have commented on how nice she is and how well she brought Harry up. In one interview on Alan Carr's *Chatty Man* Harry was asked whether the other boys fancy his mum and he got all embarrassed when they said they did, and that they thought she was amazing. Louis said, 'When we had this week at Harry's house she did come to bring us some cereal or milk, or whatever it was, in this very nice robe, I seem to remember.'

Anne gets lots of lovely messages on Twitter every day from fans asking her if she will adopt them. She has also had some nasty messages in the past from internet trolls, but she didn't let them bother her, instead tweeting: 'I hope you find inner peace.'

Harry is close to all his family and when his 84-year-old nan was ill he made sure he went to see her. His dad was in Bermuda so couldn't be there straight away. Des tweeted: 'Thanks to Harry for going to visit his nanny in hospital today. Very kind and thoughtful especially as I'm away. Thanks son x.'

A few days later he tweeted: 'Coming back tonight. Going to Bermuda airport soon. Seeing Mum weekend, she's a lot better.' Harry's dad tweets a lot. Here's a list of his top tweets:

'Joining up to follow my son Harry who is on the *X Factor*. No idea how this works really. Looking forward to getting some messages.'

'Had a great couple of hours with H last night. Still the same H despite everything. So proud and happy for all the boys. Feet on ground.'

'I did get to spend some private time with him last night which was fab! No paps, no press. Love him so much.'

'Great week! Saw Gemma and Harry yesterday. Off to Ireland on golf tour Thursday – might have a Guinness or two. Happy days!'

'1D smashed it at NBC Today programme. Had breakfast at The Carnegie Deli. Police chiefs there say crowd at studio biggest ever. So proud!'

'Having a blast going everywhere with them. Seeing the fans from INSIDE their bus is some experience.'

DID YOU KNOW?

Fans are always asking Harry to marry them and he jokingly accepts, but Harry hasn't found his future wife yet. He did, however, indirectly help a man called Brad propose to his girlfriend Emily.

Brad picked One Direction's 'One Thing' as his proposal song and on the way to a picnic with his girlfriend, he asked his friend to put on his favourite song while he was driving. The friend pressed 'play' and then Brad started miming to 'One Thing'. He parked up and then some of their friends appeared, miming to the song. As they walked, more people ran up to them or acted out some dance moves, all miming to 'One Thing'. Emily couldn't believe it – 80 of their closest friends and family took part, it was unbelievable! She was led to the nearby beach and then left alone to read special notes that Brad had left her in the sand. After reading the last note she watched an emotional video recording on a TV that had been set up, which had her family and friends telling her how special she was and how she was meant to be with Brad. He appeared behind her, got down on one knee and asked her to marry him. She said yes and then the two of them went back to where their friends and family were waiting to have a party and to see a wonderful fireworks display. To see the video, search 'Brad and Emily get Engaged' on YouTube. It's a video that would make anyone cry, so romantic!

CHAPTER 10

FAN LOVE

Harry had a few fans at school when he was the lead singer of White Eskimo but nothing prepared him for the number of fans he was going to get the second his first audition was shown on TV. Girls loved his hair, his looks, his personality and his singing voice straight away – he was the complete package.

Harry loves being able to interact with fans on Twitter and likes sending tweets to let people know what he's been up to. In the sixth week of the *X Factor* live shows, many fans turned up at the studio because he had tweeted to say they should come down to meet One Direction and the other groups that would be there that night. 'Can't wait to meet JLS, Westlife and Take That. Everyone should come down on Sunday,' he tweeted. And similarly, Louis tweeted: 'Sooooo excited to meet Take That, JLS and Westlife, hopefully gonna come out as a group to meet all the fans outside the studio!!' Any fans who could get to the studio did, so there were many people there, shouting Harry's name and hoping to get an autograph, not to mention fans of the other boys – JLS, Westlife and Take That.

All the boys love their fans so much that they have become more than fans: they are part of the 1D family. Harry's fans will do anything to get close to their favourite singer. They will scale trees so they can see over the crowds, try to rip down security fencing, pretend to be someone they're not to try and sneak in – some fans have tried some pretty crazy stunts. But Harry prefers fans to act rationally; he doesn't want any of them injuring themselves just to see him and the others.

Harry believes the dedication that some fans show is just amazing – waiting for hours in the freezing cold, just to catch a glimpse of One Direction. Even though the guys in the band have been famous for quite a while they still feel like pinching themselves. They don't feel like celebrities and are shocked when they arrive at airports in countries they've never been to before and see crowds of fans with banners.

Sometimes fans overstep the mark, though. Harry's mum Anne was very upset in July 2012 when a fan tweeted a photo of Harry's birth certificate. In a tweet she asked the fan: 'Why would you even have that??'

She didn't think something so private should be made public. The fan took down the photo straight away and apologised, tweeting: 'Sorry didn't intend to cause offence, you can get any record on the internet, nothing is private anymore, sorry x.'

The poor fan only posted it up because she wanted to prove that Harry wasn't born Harold, but some people just wouldn't

Since the UK *X Factor* auditions, Harry has come a long way. Singing on the *Today Show* in New York, USA.

Where it all began. After auditioning as a solo artist for *The X Factor*, Harry was asked to join four other boys to make up the band One Direction.

Above: As part of the *X Factor* final, the boys visited their hometowns. One Direction visiting Harry's hometown Holmes Chapel, Cheshire.

Below: Fans waiting outside Harry's house to show their support.

Catapulted into
success.

Award shows
and accolades
in abundance.

Harry receiving
BBC Radio 1's
Teen Awards in
London, 2012.

Above: Posing with their Brit Award, London 2012.

Below: Nickelodeon's 25th Annual Kids Choice Awards, Los Angeles 2012.

Harry gets to travel all over the world and experience lots of exciting things. Pulling faces with Kat the koala during One Direction's Australian tour.

When he can, Harry likes to relax and unwind.

Above: Looking comfy in his onesie with Louis, Zayn, Liam and Niall.

Below left: With friend Nick Grimshaw at the Brit Award after party.

Below right: Relaxing on a boat in Sydney, Australia. Harry's never been shy about taking his top off!

Doing what he loves the most: performing on stage.

drop it and sent horrible messages to her. She pleaded with them to stop in a tweet, saying: 'Can we just move on from the posts last night now, I've said sorry + deleted so just stop with the hate please?'

In February every year since joining One Direction, Harry receives sackloads of birthday cards from fans from around the world. He gets thousands of tweets too, and countless presents. Of course he gets lots of fan mail on a normal day but even more around his birthday and Christmas. Fans have made Harry wonderful scrapbooks and bracelets and bought him teddies, clothes, sweets and many more things. One fan sent him a photo of carrots made to look like One Direction, another sent five actual mushrooms, which had been customised to look like Harry, Zayn, Niall, Liam and Louis.

DID YOU KNOW?

On his 18th birthday there were over 50 trending topics about Harry on the internet!

Harry has signed so many autographs, in so many countries that he's lost count. He has been asked to sign some weird body parts too, as have the other members of One Direction. They told the *Daily Star*: 'A couple of fans asked us to sign their big toenails. It wasn't that gross, it was OK. I guess there are worse places to sign.'

Having a famous son is quite stressful for Harry's mum as fans are constantly knocking on her door to ask if Harry is in (even though he rarely is because he lives in London when he's not flying around the world). When he is there, he sometimes can't go out the front door because there are so many fans waiting on his street and drive. One day his friend

Will had to drive his car round to the back of his house so that Harry could jump straight in and they could make a smooth getaway, with Harry crouched down in the footwell and coats covering him. As Will drove past the fans they peeked inside but didn't realise he was one of Harry's best mates, so didn't think anything of it. Will enjoyed telling Harry that the fans had gone, so he popped his head up – only to realise that Will had fibbed. The fans chased them down the road!

In May 2012 an article in the *Sun* claimed that Harry's family had had to temporarily leave their house for a few days because Harry had come to stay and there were a lot of girls constantly standing outside. They could only move back when Harry had returned to London.

DID YOU KNOW?

One day, when the boys were in America, a fan decided to dress in an outfit identical to one that Louis' girlfriend had worn before; she did her hair just like her and put on glasses so that she could try and get close to the boys. Some fans thought it really was Eleanor and posed for photos with the imposter. It wasn't until Louis and the real Eleanor started getting tweets from fans saying how much they had enjoyed meeting Eleanor that they realised! It was very freaky.

One of Harry's celebrity fans is Robbie Williams, who sang a duet with One Direction in *The X Factor* final. After One Direction conquered America in 2012, he admitted that he was quite jealous because that was something Take That had never managed to do. He told the *Sun*: 'I see Harry through bitter-getting-old-and-married-and-can't-do-all-of-that-anymore eyes. Also, I've got a lot of love for him and One Direction.

'On the pie chart, the love outweighs the bitterness – but the bitterness is in there too.'

Robbie used to do crazy things when he was starting out, but back then no one had camera phones or Twitter. Now there is nowhere Harry can go without being photographed. Twitter is a great tool for fans who want to keep up-to-date with what Harry is doing, but sometimes the wrong information can be spread and this may leave fans feeling disappointed – for example, if they think Harry is going to be somewhere only for him to be hundreds of miles away. This happened in December 2011 when a rumour circulating on Twitter said that Harry would be turning on the Christmas lights in Knutsford, which is only 15 minutes away from his home village of Holmes Chapel. Fans turned up ready to see Harry only to find that it was their local MP George Osborne turning on the lights. Some fans were so upset that they decided to boo, but it wasn't really Osborne's fault that there had been a misunderstanding!

One person in the crowd tweeted: 'Loads of teen girls turned up. Imagine their disappointment when Osborne walked out!!!' Others said: 'The screaming soon stopped when George appeared. Funny'; 'Imagine expecting teen heart throb and getting the Prince of Darkness'; 'He got booed by his own constituents!!!'

Harry had been in London that night rehearsing with One Direction but he did return to Holmes Chapel a few weeks later to take his driving test. He wanted to pass first time really badly; it had been his new year's resolution for 2012 – but he managed it early, passing on 30 December 2011. (This meant he had to think up a new one and decided instead to have 'find a special lady' as his resolution.)

Harry was taught how to drive by Kevin Wise from the Learn in a Mini driving school. The car he drove for his lessons and for his test was a red mini. After he passed, Harry waved to nearby fans to let them know. His family were so happy for him, as were Niall, Zayn, Liam and Louis.

Gemma tweeted: 'Awkward when your younger sibling passes their driving test before you... Well done@Harry_Styles! (a.k.a. My new chauffeur).'

Liam tweeted: 'Massive well done harry!!!!!! Errmmmm Can I have a lift mate?'

Niall tweeted: 'Cmon @Harry_Styles get in! Smashes his drivin test.'

DID YOU KNOW?

Harry's hair is so big that it didn't fit in the box for his photo on his driving licence!

For Christmas 2011 Harry had had a quiet one with his family, overindulging a bit on his mum's home cooking. He loves Christmas dinner and tweeted: 'I think that Pigs in Blankets shouldn't just be limited (to Christmas) they should be an all year round kind of thing.' For New Year 2012, he held a big party at his and Louis' apartment. There were 80 people there and they had a great time. In One Direction's Christmas message Niall spoke on behalf of the others, saying: 'We want to say a massive happy Christmas to every single one of you guys around the world for all your massive support. Happy Christmas, hope you have fun around Christmas time, you're the best fans in the world, we love you!'

Harry's personal New Year's message for fans was: 'Make 2012 the year that you were nice because people don't like not nice people... so be nice... all the time!! Happy New Year!! :D.'

DID YOU KNOW?

One fan asked the boys what they would do to stop themselves being eaten if there was an alien invasion. Niall said he would get Harry to drive them away (because he'd passed his test) and Liam said he would feed the aliens pizza because it tastes better!

CHAPTER 11

FAMILY AND
FRIENDS

Harry was in America on his 18th birthday, which was hard for his family as they would have liked to have been there with him. His mum tweeted: 'Happy Birthday darling! @Harry_Styles have a great day. you're very loved !!'

She also posted up a picture of some of the gifts and cards fans had sent him. They included a mug with 'I Love Girls' written on it, a woolly hat, T-shirts, Haribo sweets, a teddy bear, bracelets, Maltesers, socks with 'Mr Perfect' written on them, personalised cards, posters and a canvas with his face on it. He had so many cards, and Anne had only selected a few to show.

Harry later tweeted: 'I feel like I've woken up with suddenly more facial hair and a deeper voice. Thank you for all your lovely Birthday messages :D .xx.'

Zayn, Niall, Liam and Louis decided to prank Harry on his

birthday. They booked him a massage at the W Hotel in Los Angeles, and he went along thinking that he was going to have a nice relaxing time, but the boys had other ideas. A *Daily Star* source revealed: 'They treated Harry to a really posh body massage and pranked him halfway through. They told the spa manager the plan and while Harry was chilling out, eyes closed, in the relaxation room, the lads ran in with four buckets of iced water and drenched him.'

Poor Harry!

As soon as Harry got back to England he made sure he had a belated birthday meal with his family. But before he could do so, he had to sort out his car, as Anne explained to Radio 1: 'When he came to start his car, he'd left the lights on and the battery was completely flat.

'This Good Samaritan in a van came past and offered to help him jumpstart it. And they couldn't do it – the chap couldn't help him, but then he tried to charge him £200! I thought that was so cheeky. He was trying to charge him 200 quid and he couldn't do anything!'

Harry, Anne and Robin went for a lovely meal together at the award-winning Rosso Italian restaurant in Manchester. Photographers managed to find out he was there, so they stood outside to photograph him but he didn't mind smiling for them. He looked absolutely gorgeous in a navy blazer with rolled-up sleeves, a grey T-shirt and jeans as he walked out of the restaurant, which is owned by Manchester United star Rio Ferdinand. The restaurant tweeted that night: 'It's great to have @Harry_Styles in the building tonight! #LoveRosso.'

Harry loves the restaurant and has been there several times. While there in May 2012, he happily posed with some fans who were eating there. Afterwards one of them tweeted: 'I wanna go back to @RossoRestaurant! Re-meet Mr Styles and re-eat all the food.' Another fan missed out because she wasn't there that night, but her dad was. She tweeted: '@Harry_Styles my dad is so lucky he met you last night in @RossoRestaurant gutted i wasnt there:(.'

Harry took Louis with him on that occasion and tweeted afterwards to say thanks: '@RossoRestaurant thanks for having me last night great to see you again old friend.' Louis also tweeted, saying: 'Lovely meal at Rosso Manchester! Great restaurant that.'

On another occasion Harry and Louis were invited to the restaurant by Rio Ferdinand himself after they'd been to see Manchester United play Stoke City at Old Trafford (Man U won 2-1). Harry and Louis are huge Man U fans and had been in the players' lounge when they got chatting. Rio wanted to update his Twitter followers so he tweeted: 'Just in the lounge with the One Direction young guns, they seem to be loving this boyband life.'

They then headed to the restaurant for something to eat. While they were there a swing singer called Cole Page started to entertain the diners. Cole wanted Harry and Louis to sing something with him but they didn't want to. No one could blame them – it was their night off, after all. Cole told the *Manchester Evening News*: 'After my main set I did a few Billy Joel songs and they came over to say they loved them. I did ask them to join me for a song but they declined. They seemed like great guys – they may be young but they're quite mature.'

Rio thought that the girls in the restaurant fancied Harry and afterwards tweeted him to say: 'The few chics that were in Rosso were all over ya!'

As well as having a meal out with his family for his birthday Harry also had a birthday meal in London with his celebrity friends. It was organised by Radio 1 DJ Nick Grimshaw, one of his closest celebrity friends, and was held at Shoreditch House, a private members' club in east London. The club has a swimming pool on the roof and a bowling alley. Pixie Geldof, the daughter of Irish singer and political activist Bob Geldof, was there. The press reported that Harry spent a lot of the night chatting to Pixie, and because of this she received quite a few nasty tweets from some fans, telling her to stay away. Harry hates it when this happens because he wants to be able to chat to girls without them getting vile abuse on Twitter.

DID YOU KNOW?

Harry tweeted Nick [Grimshaw] on 21 December 2011 to say: '@grimmers I hear I'm coming to yours for Christmas... is your dad gonna call me Henry Stars again?'

Harry didn't end up going to Nick's for Christmas; he went home to Holmes Chapel instead. Harry's favourite Christmas movie is *Miracle on 34th Street* and his favourite Christmas song is 'Have Yourself a Merry Little Christmas'.

When it was Nick's birthday they went for a meal at the La Bodega Negra restaurant in Soho and then on to the nearby Groucho Club. Caroline Flack was there, as was supermodel Kate Moss, Tulisa, Mark Ronson, Sadie Frost, Noel Fielding, Richard Bacon and Jaime Winstone.

A few days later Harry and Nick caught up again and went to Primrose Hill, northwest London to enjoy some sunshine with a group of their friends. They had some ice cream and Harry put on a muscle morphsuit (like a grown up version of a babygro), which made him look very scary when his face was covered. Nick couldn't help but laugh and take some photos; it was a great disguise as no one would have known it was Harry if they hadn't seen him put it on. Some photographers had seen him do

---

it, though, so they took some photos and the next day they appeared online. The website that sells the muscle morph quickly sold out as fans rushed to buy it.

As well as DJ Nick Grimshaw, Harry is also close to the boy band JLS. When Marvin Humes was getting married to The Saturdays singer Rochelle Wiseman in July 2012, Harry was invited. He couldn't make the stag do in Las Vegas because of work commitments in Los Angeles, but he bumped into Marvin at the airport just before his flight and gave him a big hug.

Harry and Marvin are good friends and he's always welcome at Marvin's house. Rochelle revealed to *Heat* what happened one night when Harry came round. 'I remember one time Harry fell asleep in my dog's bed!' she said 'The boys were all at our house having a party and having a great time.

'Marvin BlackBerried me a photo and there was a body asleep in our Yorkshire Terrier Tiger's bed. It was Harry! In there on his own, having a nap in the dogs bed, all curled up.'

On the actual wedding day at the gorgeous Blenheim Palace Harry was there, along with Rochelle's Saturdays' bandmates, Liam, Niall, Olly Murs and Alexandra Burke. Olly tweeted: 'The big day for Marvin & Rochelle has arrived!! Looking forward to it! Got me 'whistle & flute' pressed & clean. #loveweddings.'

DID YOU KNOW?

If the boys had to impress a girl with their dance moves, Harry would do a slide on his knees, Niall would copy some moves from JLS' 'She Makes Me Wanna' video and

> Zayn would do a triple backflip (even though he hasn't quite mastered that move yet).

Harry decided to just wear some smart black trousers and a white shirt without a tie, but Niall and Liam wore black ties. The next day Harry, who was staying at the Feathers Hotel, decided to go for a walk around Oxford, wearing a grey T-shirt with 'Lover' on the pocket. He spotted a bride in her wedding dress and went over to wish the happy couple all the best and gave her a kiss. At the time he seemed rather tired, but then the wedding had gone on until the early hours.

DID YOU KNOW?

The One Direction boys sometimes have breakfast with Marvin, Aston Merrygold, Oritsé Williams and J.B. Gill or meet up for drinks or to play golf. Harry knows he can contact the JLS boys if ever he needs advice and they'll be happy to give it. He once rang Aston for advice when he had a sore throat and was told to 'shut up' and not to talk so that he could rest his voice.

In July 2012, Harry, Aston and Olly Murs went clubbing together, with Aston tweeting: 'Smurf, Styles and Merrygold 1st team night out!! Let's get on it!! @ollyofficial @Harry_Styles BOSH Ax.'

That same day Harry and the rest of One Direction had been playing JLS at golf after their management company Modest arranged it, and Harry came out on top, winning a gold medal. Olly Murs had been there too but he hadn't wanted to play, instead tweeting: 'Didn't play!! But I'm having free dinner BOOM.'

Although Harry has other celebrity friends too, he doesn't brag about it. 'Harry has loads of secret celebrity phone numbers and we find out about them later,' Liam told the *Mirror*. 'We'll see something in the papers and be like, "What's going on here?" and he'll be like, "Oh, it's Gary from Take That or whoever, don't worry about it".'

Harry's cousin Ben might not be famous yet, but he could be soon as he is a singer and guitarist for the up-and-coming band Concept. Ben Selley thinks he owes his cousin Harry and One Direction a lot. He explained to the *Basingstoke Gazette*: 'When I went to see him on *X Factor* I thought I would never be able to do that. But I sat in my room playing guitar and getting better, and then realising I can sing.

'I don't really like to use Harry as in, "Look, I'm Harry Styles' cousin, come and watch my band". I want my own success. But One Direction do inspire me. I still haven't got over how famous they are.'

Ben's bandmates are Karim Newton, Matt Goodenough, Nathan Gittens and Scott Dicks. They were originally a four-piece before Ben joined, and had unsuccessfully auditioned for *X Factor* in 2011. Concept is influenced by Ed Sheeran, Duran Duran, Motown and The Beatles; to find out more about them, why not follow them on Twitter @conceptofficial or join their Facebook fan page, Concept Official. Their first single '7teen' is available to download on iTunes.

CHAPTER 12

TOURING

Harry had loved *The X Factor Live Tour* but it didn't compare with the *Up All Night Tour*, which started out across the UK and Ireland and then went around the world, with more than 60 shows. Instead of singing five songs a night, he and the boys sang 15 songs. They sang songs from their album as well as five covers. The boys announced their UK and Ireland *Up All Night Tour* on 27 September 2011 and fans couldn't wait to get hold of tickets for the concerts, which were held during December 2011 and January 2102. Their first show was on 21 December in Liam's hometown of Wolverhampton before moving to Manchester, Bournemouth, Birmingham, Plymouth, Nottingham, Brighton, London, Glasgow, Liverpool, Newcastle, Blackpool, Sheffield, Cardiff and Dublin, ending in Belfast on 26 January.

As soon as the tickets were available to buy fans snapped them up, with people panicking on Twitter because they'd heard a rumour that all 21 dates had sold out in 10.6 seconds! Ticket touts took advantage, putting tickets on eBay for £100 each. The *Up All Night* set list was fantastic. Here is a list of the songs that the boys played:

1. 'Na Na Na'
2. 'Stand Up'
3. 'I Wish'
4. Medley: 'I Gotta Feeling' / 'Stereo Hearts' / 'Valerie' / 'Torn'
5. 'Moments'
6. 'Gotta Be You'
7. 'More than This'
8. 'Up All Night'
9. 'Tell Me a Lie'
10. 'Everything About You'
11. 'Use Somebody'
12. 'One Thing'
13. 'Save You Tonight'
14. 'What Makes You Beautiful'
Encore
'I Want'

Before the tour started they did two warm-up gigs to try things out and check that everything worked. One of the gigs was at Watford Colosseum in London. Richard Brazier, marketing assistant for the venue, was really excited about Harry, Niall, Zayn, Liam and Louis' debut in Watford, telling his local paper: 'It seems like it has been a long time since we announced it. I think it is a really big deal for us and for Watford – we are really looking forward to it.'

One Direction held a Twitter competition to give fans the opportunity to come up onstage with them and sing, and lots of fans entered. On the night itself the winners had a brilliant time, but afterwards three of them started to get hate messages on Twitter, criticising their looks. Because of this the decision was made that One Direction wouldn't be able to invite any more fans on stage during the tour.

Hollie Gilbert, one of the winners, told the *Sunday Mirror*, 'I was partnered with Harry. Then they sang to us wearing tuxes. Harry was really sweet. The jealous messages began almost straight away. I think it's because I was partnered with Harry, the most popular member.'

The boys' spokesman released a statement, saying: 'The girls were brought up on stage for a warm-up show at the beginning of the tour as a try. It didn't work out from a practical point of view.'

Thousands of fans came to watch every performance and Harry was always buzzing when he came offstage. The boys recorded some backstage videos to let fans know how it was going and in one Harry said, 'I think for us the highlights of the tour have been the audiences. The audiences have been just so enthusiastic and really got involved. So it's been good that they've been a part of the whole show, the whole experience. It's been great.'

For Harry touring is the best thing about being a pop star and he is so grateful for the support of all One Direction fans.

Niall's favourite performance of the *Up All Night* UK and Ireland tour was their show in Dublin. He was so excited beforehand, tweeting: 'IRELAND we are coming... been waiting for this day all my life!' and 'I cannot wait! Lets pull the roof off the O2 tomorrow night!'

On the morning of their performance he tweeted: 'Today

is a very special day for me! I literally cannot wait! #1DinDublin.'

Afterwards, he told fans: 'Ireland! Absolutely incredible is an understatement!'

'Thank you for a lovely welcome home! Had goosebumps all night and a tear in my eye!' and '#Irishandproud small nation but we can sure make a hell of a lot of noise! Love you all! Dream come true.'

Another big night for the boys was their final evening in London on 22 January 2012. They had loved performing at the HMV Apollo, with Zayn tweeting: 'London!! Smashed it amazing show thank you' and 'Directioners never fail to impress me with there [sic] lung capacity u guys can scream! #amazingfans!'

Niall tweeted: 'London incredible tonight! Off t chill now! Cant wait t sleep.'

One of their most memorable nights during the tour was their performance at the Hammersmith Apollo on 22 January, known by fans as #1DstagegotraidedFAM (as in, stage got raided). One fan managed to get on stage with them while they were singing 'I Want'. She started dancing behind the table before being chased by security. The fan's Twitter name is @BeckySaless and she has over 20,000 followers. Harry tweeted #1DstagegotraidedFAM and it trended worldwide.

As they started to gain fans around the world, the boys were told that their *Up All Night* tour was to be extended to Australia and New Zealand, with dates in Sydney, Brisbane, Melbourne, Auckland and Wellington in April 2012. This was a dream come true for Liam, who had tweeted just months earlier: 'I want to tour more everywhere all over the world I'm gunna miss touring when this one finishes #worldtour. Because I haven't big massive shout out to our British fans you made this tour amazing.'

On 21 March 2012 the American leg of the *Up All Night* tour was announced. Harry and the boys would be performing all around North America for 26 dates in May and June, finishing on 1 July in Florida. One of the supporting acts was an old friend, Olly Murs, who had come second in the 2009 series of *X Factor.* The Filipino-American singer Manika also supported them, and her dressing room was right next to theirs. Harry and the boys taught her some slang words that she'd never heard before, like chin-wag. She was shocked at how devoted some Directioners are, checking into the hotels the boys stay at on the offchance of bumping into them in the lift or the restaurant. In one interview she confessed that Zayn likes to wear two pairs of socks at once and that he used to drive a mini-scooter from their dressing room to the canteen rather than walk. If you want to follow Manika on Twitter you can: @Manikaofficial.

In an interview with *Infelicious.com* Manika was asked whether she got to hang out with One Direction and she replied, 'Yes, they're all such sweet guys. Actually, at yesterday's show [in Chicago] they got these golf carts, and then I have this mini scooter. It was kind of scary. I didn't do it because I was scared of like breaking my leg, but they were driving the golf cart while some were riding on the back of the scooter holding on. They also like to throw water so I almost got wet. I was like, "You guys, my hair does not get water poured [on it]!"

'And they have these Nerf guns, and you'll be trying to do sound check, and they'll be shooting them in the background. They're a bunch of fun, like really, really sweet, down-to-earth guys.'

Harry and the boys were offered the opportunity to support

Big Time Rush on their *Better With U* tour after their own tour finished and they jumped at the chance. Big Time Rush is an American boy band with a hit Nickelodeon TV show of the same name. Kendall Schmidt, James Maslow, Carlos Pena Jr. and Logan Henderson enjoyed hanging out with One Direction, as they revealed in an interview with *Sugarscape*. 'They were really cool, we met them and they kind of have the same humour as us and I think we're going to get into a little trouble on tour... good trouble,' they said, adding that if Harry or one of the others wanted to strip off that would be fine because each band was going to have its own tour bus. They imagined they'd be like big brothers as they are all 21 or older.

When One Direction arrived in Toronto, Canada ready for the Big Time Rush gig they had on 26 February, they were confronted by thousands of screaming fans. They had an interview lined up on the *Much Music* TV show and the fans all wanted to meet them, so had turned up at the studio because they knew the boys would be performing on a stage that was set up outside. There were so many fans that officials had to close the street! One fan threw a pink bra at Louis and he responded by saying, 'I don't think it will fit.'

After they'd been touring around the world for quite a few months Harry and the rest of One Direction decided to record a special message for their UK and Irish fans. In it Harry said, 'Hi guys, we just wanted to put out a quick message to tell you how much we miss you in the UK and Ireland. We wanna say thank you so much for all your support while we've been away and we cannot wait to come home and see you guys.'

One Direction released a DVD of their tour in May 2012 so that fans who hadn't been able to get tickets could experience what the *Up All Night* tour was like. It also allowed all the fans to see what went on behind the scenes in rehearsals and in the dressing room. They planned a special Live Twitter DVD watch party and invited fans from around the world to take part. All they had to do was watch the DVD at 5pm (London time) on 31 May and they could see live updates from the boys on Twitter as they watched. Niall was so impressed when he found out there were thousands of people taking part. He tweeted: 'This is crazy! 1800 of you guys in the Philippines went out to watch the tour DVD all together! Thank you soo much.'

In February 2012 the boys announced they would be doing a UK and Ireland Arena tour in 2013. Initially there were only going to be 15 dates, starting at the O2 Arena in London on 22 February and calling at Glasgow, Cardiff, Belfast, Manchester, Liverpool, Sheffield, Nottingham and Birmingham before finishing at Newcastle Metro Radio Arena on 24 March. The tickets sold out minutes after going on sale at 9am on Saturday, 25 February so the boys tweeted that more dates would be added. They ended up adding another 20 dates because the demand for tickets was so high!

The band announced in April 2012 that they would be doing a summer arena tour in America and Canada after the UK tour. It would start in Florida on 13 June and end on 8 August in Los Angeles.

DID YOU KNOW?

One of the bodyguards for the American and Canada dates was to be Michael Jackson's former bodyguard, Alberto Alvarez. 'I'm really excited,' he told the *People*. 'They're a great group of young men and they have great talent. I am proud to work for them. Working for the boys has pulled me through a terrible time. It really helped me cope with what happened three years ago when Michael died.'

He added, 'Working for One Direction – the biggest boy band in the world – is so exciting. I did some work for them in California last year and they liked me. Now every time they are here, I work with them. The other week I was with Zayn Malik at the Video Music Awards in Los Angeles. A few months back I spent time with Louis Tomlinson and his girlfriend.'

Despite being a huge star around the world, Harry hasn't changed at all. When he's away his mum misses him like crazy but they catch up as soon as he lands back in England. 'I do worry about Harry, as any mum would,' Anne told *Heat* magazine. 'But so far it's been amazing the way he's taken it all in his stride and remained so grounded.

'He's a mummy's boy sometimes, he phones up to five times a day. When there's a time difference, he tends to text saying, "I love you, Mum" or "I miss you". He's still my little boy.'

Anne has been out to visit him a lot while he's been touring America and the rest of the world, but she isn't the only one. Harry invited his dad to come out and see him when he was in New York. Des couldn't believe how many fans came to see One Direction when they were performing on the *Morning Show* on NBC – there were over 15,000! He really rates Niall, Liam, Zayn and Louis and loves how they all get on so well; he loved spending time with them in their tour van.

To keep up to date with what Harry is doing Des uses Twitter and Harry texts him, too. On Father's Day 2012 Harry was in America so he sent his dad a tweet and Gemma took round some wine from them both.

Harry never expected to have so many American fans and for their music to be so popular there. He confessed to *ABC*

News: 'We're just five normal boys from the UK who've been given this opportunity, so we're having a great time working very hard.'

For months leading up to their arrival in the States, social media was used to get people excited and to build a fan base for them. Harry thinks a lot of their success comes from this. 'Twitter, Facebook and YouTube have been a large percentage of the reason we've been known outside of the UK,' he explained. 'We owe a massive thank you to the fans.'

They set up a website called Bring 1D to US (www.bring1dtous.com) and encouraged people to take part in challenges. In a statement on their website they said:

Are you ready to Bring 1D to your city? Visit www.Bring1DtoUS.com now to get started on the first challenge. Click on your city for directions about how you can earn points for your city. Each challenge will bring you one step closer to a special 1D event in your city! We'll be awarding points after the completion of the challenges in the following way:

1st place = 100 points
2nd place = 80 points
3rd place = 60 points
4th place = 40 points
5th place = 20 points

If you don't see your city on the map, enter the challenge as a wildcard city for a chance to be added later. We'll be paying attention to who's participating; if your city makes a big splash, we'll be taking notice.

Stay tuned for weekly updates. We'll also be adding fun bonus challenges out there.

Best of luck!

The city that won was Dallas in Texas and the boys made their special trip on 24 March 2012. They had planned on going to the Stonebriar Centre Mall but so many fans wanted to go that they moved it to the larger Dr. Pepper Ballpark. Fans could get a signed copy of *Up All Night* and watch One Direction perform one song. Thousands of fans showed up, it was crazy!

CHAPTER 13

SPECIAL MOMENTS

Harry will never forget performing 'What Makes You Beautiful' at the BBC Radio 1 Teen Awards in October 2011 and the *Jingle Bell Ball* in December 2011. The boys were also invited to perform at *The X Factor* 2011 final. It was great to return to the show that brought them together, and performing the song as a medley with JLS and their song 'She Makes Me Wanna' was such a privilege. Both bands had failed to win *X Factor* but both have done phenomenally well ever since. The final was held at Wembley Stadium and the atmosphere was intense when they performed.

The following year brought international performances of 'What Makes You Beautiful' – Harry loved performing at the 2012 Sanremo Music Festival in Italy, on *The Today Show* and 2012 *Kids Choice Awards* in America, and at the *Logie Awards* in

Australia. One Direction's biggest performance was without question at the 2012 Olympics Closing Ceremony in London, which was watched by four billion people!

To top it all, One Direction sang 'What Makes You Beautiful' on top of a lorry as it circled the inside of the Olympic Stadium; they followed 80s bands Madness and the Pet Shop Boys. Zayn debuted a new hairstyle for this event – a blond band in his quiff – and all five boys looked like they were having the time of their lives. Afterwards Niall tweeted: 'That was unbelievable, highlight of our career, and the biggest audience we will ever play to 1 billion people! #ThankYouLondon2012.'

DID YOU KNOW?

Before their performance the boys decided to sneak off from their security team and explore the Olympic Park on their own. They had all-access passes, so managed to get a ride to the top of the Orbit Tower, even though they didn't have tickets, and they went to the Aquatics Centre even though it was closed to the public at the time. They even got to watch some of the water polo – and teased their security team by sending them photos. The band met the Spice Girls and Liam managed to kiss Mel B, Mel C, Geri and Emma on the cheek!

Another highlight for Harry was getting to act in the hit Nickelodeon show, *iCarly*. The studio where the show is filmed in Los Angeles was surrounded by more than 500 fans, who started lining up to meet them 12 hours before they arrived. *iCarly* is a sitcom about a girl called Carly Shay (played by Miranda Cosgrove), who has her own web show with her friends, Freddie and Sam (their show is called *iCarly*). Harry and the boys appeared in the second episode in season six, 'iGo One Direction', and 3.9 million people watched it in the States alone when it was screened on 7 April 2012.

The official episode synopsis explained their part: 'Carly returns home sick after a trip and discovers that One Direction has accepted an invitation to perform on their web show. Not long after arriving, bandmate Harry becomes sick and we see Carly doting over him. Realizing Harry is playing sick for the attention, they hatch a plan to get him back in the group by telling him Gibby has become their newest bandmember. Meanwhile, Spencer becomes a personal trainer and gives a bratty girl a makeover.'

The boys did a really good job and the actresses and actors involved were more than impressed. Miranda Cosgrove told Clevver TV, 'Their accents are really amazing and they're really nice guys so it was fun. It was their first time acting and they got to sing one of their songs on the show, so it was cool to hear them sing.'

The band was surprised when rumours claiming that they had been offered their own TV series by Nickelodeon started up, but they explained in interviews that this wasn't the case. Niall told a radio host from CKO196.9 Radio: 'Since we said we were coming to America, Nickelodeon have been right with us from the start y'know, they helped us out, y'know, we hosted their Saturday night TV shows for the whole month of March, we did an episode of *iCarly*. They're giving us the biggest performance at the Kids Choice Awards next week and us and Katy Perry are the only people performing, so it's very much a big deal. Nickelodeon have been really good to us but there's no TV show.'

Harry has lots of tattoos, and he's constantly adding to his collection, so when he performs you can often see a few of them on his arms. Some of the tattoos he keeps hidden and he doesn't reveal the meaning behind them but others he is happy to share. They have special meanings. He's got the lyrics 'won't stop till we surrender' from group The Temper Trap's track 'Sweet Disposition' tattooed on his arm, underneath his star tattoo on his left bicep. He also has the letter 'A', which is for his mum Anne and was drawn by Zayn. He has '17 Black', which is a gambling number used by James Bond, a coat hanger, 'Hi' (which fans think was written by Louis), 'I can't change' inked around his wrist, an iced gem because that was his sister's nickname when she was younger, comedy and tragedy drama masks, a birdcage with SCML underneath it... the list goes on. Harry loves tattoos and he couldn't wait to get a half sleeve.

DID YOU KNOW?

There is no meaning behind Harry's star tattoo; he just knew that he wanted a tattoo there, and decided on a star. When fans saw the SCML tattoo they wondered if it was for Simon Cowell, or if it stood for 'Smile Now, Cry Later', but Harry has never revealed what it really means.

One of the tattoo artists Harry has used is Kevin Paul, who has also done tattoos for Aston Merrygold from JLS, Rizzle Kicks, Ed Sheeran and actor Paddy Considine. Harry decided that he was the tattoo artist he wanted to do his half sleeve. Kevin's Twitter account is @kevinp666. One fan tweeted: 'Hi,@kevinp666 can you please answer, did @Harry_Styles delete his tattoo "won't stop 'till we surrender"?' Kevin replied: 'No it was just done bad so it's really faded.'

DID YOU KNOW?

Niall doesn't have any tattoos but if he did ever get one it would probably be a barcode on his arm.

Harry asked Kevin to draw something from his childhood and another image, but Kevin is sworn to secrecy and won't reveal what it is to the media. Ed Sheeran came with Harry when he went to Kevin's studio and drew a little padlock tattoo on Harry's wrist (there is a photo of him doing it on the internet).

DID YOU KNOW?

Ed and One Direction love messing around and one day when they were in the studio in his house they decided to have a food fight and started throwing bits of watermelon at each other. They ended up picking up Harry and putting him in the melon! One Direction have always loved having fruit fights and play fruit ninja in their dressing rooms – they throw fruit up in the air and slice it while in the air. They don't recommend fans copy them in case they hurt themselves, though.

CHAPTER 14

TAKE
ME HOME

When the boys were in Los Angeles working on their second album Harry decided to rent a luxury car to get around in. Even though he had only passed his test six months earlier he decided to rent a black Ferrari California convertible, which would cost £120,000 ($195,000) to buy. The rent alone for one day is roughly £1,300 ($2,200), so he racked up quite a substantial bill.

Harry loves to drive expensive cars and he has two cars in London: a Range Rover Sport and an Audi R8 Coupé. When he got his Range Rover Sport the press reported that the insurance alone was £15,000 because of his age and the fact that he had just passed his test and was a pop star. His dad Des gave him some advice when he started out – that for every £10 he earns, he should spend £6 or £7 wisely. Harry sticks to this and has fun with the rest. For Harry, driving expensive cars is really fun.

> **DID YOU KNOW?**
>
> When Harry was driving his Range Rover in London one day he got squirted in the face with water pistols when he pulled up at some traffic lights. He told BBC Radio 1 DJ Scott Mills, 'It was the weirdest thing – they were like these two grown men. I felt so degraded afterwards.'

Harry loved having the opportunity to record some more of Ed Sheeran's songs for the boys' second album, *Take Me Home*. Before they headed to the studio Ed revealed their plans to the *Daily Star*, saying, 'I wrote a couple of songs when I was 17 that One Direction want for their next album. I'm going into the studio in August to produce the tracks for them.' He was adamant that he wouldn't be singing on any of the tracks because their music styles were so different. Ed revealed what fans should expect: 'Seventeen-year-old Ed just wrote a lot of love songs, so expect to hear a lot of love songs on their album, I guess.' He was dating a really nice girl back then and she inspired him to write lots of ballads.

> **DID YOU KNOW?**
>
> Harry briefly appears in Ed's video for his song 'Drunk'.

To get to work with Ed was a huge honour for the One Direction boys. Louis said, 'He's just one of the best lyricists of our generation, so having the chance to work with him is amazing,' they told Capital Radio. 'It was really important for us. His method recording wise – you just do a couple of takes because he likes to keep it really raw and really real.'

Zayn added, 'He's got a field and sometimes you just sit out on the field and jam with a guitar, play a little bit of football, walk into the studio when you feel like it, walk back out when you feel like it. It's wicked.'

One day after they'd been working in the studio all day, and even though it was pretty late, Harry and Ed decided to go to the V Festival in Chelmsford, Essex because Harry's friend had two spare tickets. They got a taxi there and arrived at 10pm, thinking it would go on till 6am. Ed explained to the *Sun*, 'But it finishes really early and everyone was coming out as we were waiting around for Harry's mate with our tickets. We ended up hiding behind a Pizza Express truck for half an hour until his mate came, then when we got in, it was all over. We eventually got back to Harry's at 4am and I slept on his floor.'

Ed's a really good friend of Harry's and our favourite pop star decided to pull a prank on him one day. He managed to get hold of a video of Ed when he was a schoolboy in a production of *Grease*. Harry tweeted some stills from the video with the message: 'Just casually watching @edsheeran playing 'Roger' in Grease…

'Intimate moment with Lily and Ed. If anyone was wondering, he is the mooning champ of Rydell high. And sings the mooning song beautifully.'

His tweets were retweeted over 16,000 times, so soon the photos were all over the world. He teased Ed further by putting: '@edsheeran if you're ever mean to me, I have the video of you dancing to 'Go Grease Lightning' do you think anyone would like to see that?'

One of his fans tweeted: '@Harry_Styles stop bullying @edsheeran.'

To which Harry replied: 'I can't help it... there's too many videos of thrusting.'

When Ed saw what Harry had done he replied with a tweet just saying '@HarryStyles my dad likes you.'

On another occasion Harry tweeted: 'I feel left out because @louis_Tomlinson and @edsheeran have a bond over olives.' The next day he decided to make Ed's face out of vegetables and tweeted it to fans. It had carrots for his hair, roast potatoes for eyes, a green bean for his nose and a parsnip for his mouth.

Harry honestly believes that the songs on *Take Me Home* are better than the tracks on their first album and he is so glad that fans love the album too. Harry wants to keep on making amazing music with One Direction for many years to come. He told the *Mirror*: 'Naturally, I wonder how long it will last. But we get on so well I can't see us having a massive bust-up or anything like that.'

Why don't you flip over the book and read *Niall Horan: The Biography*?

NIALL HORAN

THE BIOGRAPHY

SARAH OLIVER

JOHN BLAKE

Published by John Blake Publishing Ltd,
3 Bramber Court, 2 Bramber Road,
London W14 9PB, England

www.johnblakepublishing.co.uk

www.facebook.com/Johnblakepub facebook
twitter.com/johnblakepub twitter

First published in paperback in 2013

ISBN: 978 1 78219 220 6

British Library Cataloguing-in-Publication Data:

A catalogue record for this book is available from the British Library.

Design by www.envydesign.co.uk

Printed and bound in Great Britain by CPI Group (UK) Ltd

1 3 5 7 9 10 8 6 4 2

Papers used by John Blake Publishing are natural, recyclable products made
from wood grown in sustainable forests. The manufacturing processes
conform to the environmental regulations of the country of origin.

Every attempt has been made to contact the relevant copyright-holders,
but some were unobtainable. We would be grateful if the
appropriate people could contact us.

DEDICATION

Dedicated with love to my aunties and uncles: Anne, Bob, Fay, Helen, Howard, Ian (x2), Jill & Ste.

A big thank you to Niall's biggest fans: Sam Murphy, Ava 'B' Owens, Nyah Auger-Friel, Ruby Murphy, Lily Murphy, Bradley Milford, Max Murphy, Kirstie Milford, Maddy Page, Bethan Page, Morgan Parker, Harry Murphy, Megan Bailey and Noah Murphy.

CONTENTS

If you love Niall, follow him on Twitter at: Niall –
https://Twitter.com/NiallOfficial

Other interesting people connected to Niall, who you might
want to follow:

Niall's brother Greg – https://Twitter.com/greghoran87
Niall's cousin Daniel Horan –
https://Twitter.com/danielhoran2005
Niall's auntie Amanda Horan –
https://Twitter.com/mandylhoran
Niall's cousin Aoife Horan – https://Twitter.com/aoifehoran
Niall's cousin Sinead Horan –
https://Twitter.com/SineadHoran
Niall's friends – https://Twitter.com/seancullen95;
https://Twitter.com/williedevine
One Direction's Tour Manager Paul Higgins –
https://Twitter.com/paulyhiggins
One Direction's band drummer, Josh Devine –
https://Twitter.com/JoshDevineDrums
One Direction's band bass guitarist, Sandy Beales –
https://Twitter.com/sandybeales

One Direction's band musical director/kcys, Jon Shone –
https://Twitter.com/JonShoneKeys
One Direction band guitarist, Dan Richards –
https://Twitter.com/guitarmandan

1993: A STAR IS BORN!

Niall James Horan was born on 13 September 1993 in Mullingar, County Westmeath in Ireland. His mother Maura Gallagher and father Bobby Horan were thrilled to have a second son. He has one older brother called Greg. Niall's parent's split up when he was young, divorcing when he was five.

For a while Niall and Greg lived some of the time with their mum Maura, who lives in Edgeworthstown (half an hour's drive away from Mullingar) and some of the time with their dad Bobby, before they made the decision to live permanently with their father. It was much easier to get to school living at their dad's.

Bobby Horan is a butcher in a supermarket, which meant he sometimes had to leave for work very early, so from the age of seven Niall had to get himself up and ready for school. His dad

worked long hours so Niall was taught how to use a washing machine, how to iron his uniform and how to cook, with the help of his big brother. They would walk to school together, which was a mile and a half away. At weekends and after school Niall used to hang around with his brother a lot, even though Niall got on Greg's nerves. They would have fights but Greg generally won because he was bigger.

When he was little, Niall had an army outfit with a helmet that he liked to wear and a huge gun that was almost as big as he was. He had a fear of clowns and so he didn't like to go to birthday parties in case there was a clown there. In one video for their official YouTube channel he admitted to his bandmates that he used to have an imaginary friend called Michael when he was younger – and he used to like sandwiches without crusts!

DID YOU KNOW?

Niall used to have two birthday parties every year, one with his dad and the other with his mum.

Niall has always loved singing and when he was eight years old his teacher spotted that he was a talented singer and told him that he should put himself forward for the Mullingar choir. He also sang solo in the school choir. His family realised he could sing when they were travelling in the car together and Niall started to sing – they thought it was the radio, his voice was that good!

Niall's primary school teacher Anna Caulfield still works at St Kenny National School and remembers how talented he was at singing. Anna also thought he was very polite and had a lovely personality. She told her local paper: 'He was a little saintly child in the classroom and every other teacher would say the same. A very, very good boy.'

2

When Niall was 10 he got the performing bug after acting in a school play. He revealed all to the *X Factor* cameras: 'I've always sung and when I was about 10, I played Oliver in the school play and I just always remember being really happy onstage.'

DID YOU KNOW?

Niall has been back to visit his old primary school and the children sang 'Consider Yourself At Home' from the musical *Oliver!* and 'We'd do anything for you, Niall, anything'. Afterwards he signed autographs and answered some questions. His former principal Arthur Fallon can remember Niall playing Oliver and told a local reporter: 'I remember that song "Where is Love?", he sang that song. It's a very difficult song, and he sang it and it was very moving.'

Niall was never bullied at school and had lots of friends. He enjoyed primary school but wasn't keen on homework, preferring to have fun instead of having his head in his books. When he was 11 he started to play the guitar and was soon hooked.

Niall went to Coláiste Mhuire secondary school, which is an all-boys Christian school, and had to make new friends because his friends from primary school were put in different classes to him. His favourite teacher at the school was his French teacher, Georgina Ainscough. He loved playing sport and his best mates at school were called Nicky and Niall. They enjoying messing around and sometimes skipped lessons if they thought they could get away with it. (They did get caught once, though!)

Niall was even more into performing and so when he was 13 and found out there was to be a school talent show he

decided to go for it. He formed a duo with his friend Kieron Dowling. Kieron loved playing the guitar, too, so he played as Niall sang. They chose to sing The Script classic 'Man Who Can't Be Moved' – they did really well.

Niall also started to sing and act at the Mullingar Arts Centre. Outside of school, if he ever went to a place where there was karaoke he would sing the Frank Sinatra classic 'Fly Me To The Moon'.

Niall's dad converted the garage at the bottom of their garden into a bedroom so his son could have more space to play guitar without disturbing the neighbours. Niall decided to have two red walls and two blue walls and decorated it with football posters. He has a signed Jamie Ward Derby County poster and a signed Danny Simpson Newcastle United poster on the wall of his bedroom at his dad's house. Niall summed up how much he loves football when he tweeted on 25 August 2012: 'I love football so much! I will watch anything!'

While at school he had a Bebo profile, something he is really embarrassed about now. When fans found it he tweeted: 'Hahaha my old Bebo page, don't even know the password for that anymore! My cousin Claire came up with the stupid name #embarassin' and 'bebo page is hilarious! some great memories in the pictures though ey?'

On his Bebo profile Niall had written: 'ari everybod! the name is niall.im 16.im in 5th year in mary's. singin is my life do nothin else! im always up for a laff so if u know me or wanna know me leave uz a comment and do my blogs girls. cya later bud.'

He revealed that he's happiest 'havin a laff. oh i love eh. some buzz blarin the tunes(then the neighbours go mad).watchin derby(not always) and wi this person (no names).'

On Bebo there were some great photos but the account is now set to private so it can only be viewed by selected people.

In September 2009, Niall decided to enter a local talent show once again with his friend Kieron, who accompanied him on guitar. They performed the Chris Brown track 'With You' and the crowd went crazy; they thought Niall was amazing, joining in with him and screaming. It was unbelievable – several people rushed over at the end to ask for his autograph because they knew he would one day be famous, he was just so talented! He posed for a photo with Kieron and their trophy and looked so happy. His local paper was there to cover the event but they didn't print the story until two weeks later and even then they didn't print a photo. Niall's grandma wasn't at all happy and rang up to complain.

DID YOU KNOW?

Niall took every opportunity he could to perform and for a while he even helped out a local band.

Two months later, Niall entered the Mullingar Shamrocks' show, *Stars In Their Eyes*. He could have sung Chris Brown's 'With You' again but instead chose to sing Jason Mraz's 'I'm Yours'. Niall loved the buzz appearing onstage gave him and he started to get fans but he wasn't complacent and still practised a lot in his bedroom – he wanted to be an even better guitarist and singer.

A few weeks later, on 13 December 2009, Niall was watching *The X Factor* final (Series 6) when he decided he should enter. He had just see Joe McElderry win, and he was only 18. Niall went straight online and applied for the show. He really wanted to be a singer and winning his local talent show had given him the confidence to believe that he could one day be a professional singer. On 16 January 2010 he tweeted: 'Applied for *xfactor*, hope it all works out.' He had just

begun studying for his leaving certificate, so in an in ideal world he would have waited a year until he finished that before applying, but Niall didn't want to wait. If it didn't work out then he would carry on studying and go to university to study sound engineering.

On 31 January 2010, Niall performed at the Academy, Dublin as the warm-up act for *X Factor* star Lloyd Daniels (who finished in fifth place in *The X Factor* Series 6). It was a great honour to be asked as the organisers were looking for someone really good and Niall didn't have an agent, he was just a schoolboy. Niall sang Justin Bieber's 'Baby' and Justin Timberlake's 'Cry Me A River' in front of thousands of screaming girls. His family were 100 per cent behind him entering *The X Factor* and supported him that night too, because they knew how much singing meant to him. Niall's mum Maura summed up what her son is like during an interview with the *Westmeath Examiner*. 'He's a light-hearted lad,' she said. 'One thing I do know is that he is completely committed and focused on his singing. He'd sing for his breakfast, dinner and tea!'

DID YOU KNOW?

That night, Niall told Lloyd that he had applied for *The X Factor*.

CHAPTER 2

TIME TO SHINE

Niall auditioned for *The X Factor* 2010 at Croke Park Stadium in Dublin along with thousands of other hopefuls. He enjoys playing his guitar while he sings, so he brought it along with him and while queuing up for his *X Factor* audition he performed for the crowd, singing Justin Bieber's 'One Time'. He loves entertaining people and impressed the girls waiting in the line next to him. There were thousands of people queuing up but the girls decided to film Niall singing on their phone. To see the video, just search 'Niall Horan One Time' on YouTube. You'll see his brother standing next to him (Greg doesn't seem to be paying Niall much attention – he'd probably heard him sing that song hundreds of times). Back then, Niall was hoping he would progress through the competition so that he could get attention from good-

looking girls, make an album, go on tour and sing on live TV every week!

When Niall reached the front of the queue he had to audition in front of *X Factor* staff first. After putting in a good performance, he was told to come back the next day. He then had another two auditions in front of the staff and was interviewed by *X Factor* host Dermot O'Leary. Before auditioning Niall probably had no idea how hard it was going to be; he had to impress three times and they still wouldn't say whether he'd been chosen to sing in front of the actual judges! They just told him to go home and they would contact him. Weeks passed and Niall heard nothing. About a month later he was on holiday in Spain when he got the phone call he'd been waiting for – he had been chosen to audition in front of Simon Cowell, Cheryl Cole, Louis Walsh and Katy Perry. It's a good job he took his cell phone on holiday with him!

Once he arrived home in Mullingar, Niall had to get his audition outfit ready for 28 June: a red, green and white checked shirt, with a green T-shirt underneath, jeans and trainers. His look summed him up: it was cheeky and casual. There was no way he could have auditioned in a smart suit – he had to be true to himself.

In Niall's chat to the backstage cameras he sounded pretty confident that he would do well and explained that he'd been compared to Justin Bieber in the past. 'I want to sell out arenas, and make an album and work with some of the best artists in the world,' he declared. 'Today is the start of it all – if I get through today, it's game on!'

When he walked onstage Niall said, 'Alright Dublin, alright guys!' He was smiling away and showing off his playful side. After he had revealed his name, Louis Walsh asked why he was auditioning. Niall said that he wanted to be the best artist he

could be in the world. Unlike Harry, who had to audition in front of Louis, Nicole Scherzinger and Simon Cowell, Niall had four judges to impress: Louis, Simon, Cheryl Cole and Katy Perry. The audience wolf-whistled, took to their feet and cheered him, but the judges were not convinced that his performance of Ne-Yo's 'So Sick' was good enough. Here's their first reaction:

Katy Perry: 'I think you're adorable! You've got charisma – I just think that maybe you should work on that. You're only 16: I started out when I was 15 and I didn't make it until I was 23.'

Simon Cowell: 'I think you're unprepared – I think you came with the wrong song, you're not as good as you thought you were, but I still like you.'

Cheryl Cole: 'Yeah, you're obviously adorable. You've got a lot of charm for a 16-year-old, but the song's too big for you, babe.'

Louis Walsh: 'Niall, I think you've got something. I think that people would absolutely like you because you're likeable.'

When it came to voting, Simon said 'yes', Cheryl was a 'no', and then Louis butted in with a 'yes' before Katy could cast her vote (he guessed that she was going to say no, but causing her to vote last would make her decide Niall's fate). Louis told her, 'I wanted to give him a chance... he needs three yeses.' This proved a very clever move because Katy now felt torn. She told Niall, 'Can I just say that I agree with Cheryl, you do need more experience and, by the way, just if you're likeable, likeableness does not sell records – it's talent and you have a seed of it. Of course you're in!'

As soon as Niall heard Katy say he was in, he jumped in the air before rushing off to see his family and have a big group hug. Katy's final words to him were, 'Don't let us down!'

Niall's audition wasn't shown on the *X Factor*'s main show

but was instead aired on the *Xtra Factor*, which suggests that *X Factor* bosses weren't expecting him to make the live shows. Only Harry and Liam's auditions were shown on the main show, with Zayn and Louis' auditions only shown after the *X Factor* final. Niall and Liam were the only members of One Direction to face four judges; the others only had three to try and impress.

For Niall, going to bootcamp was a huge deal because he nearly missed out. If Katy Perry had been allowed to vote before Louis, he would probably have got two yeses and two nos. He had to practise even more than usual because only the best singers would make it from bootcamp to the judges' houses round. Flying from Dublin all the way to London without his family to support him, he must have felt out of his comfort zone. At bootcamp there were more than 200 singers, so he would have to excel in his performances if he was to stand out from the crowd.

When he arrived at Wembley, Niall was told to go with the other boys and rehearse Michael Jackson's 'Man In The Mirror'. The judges had chosen one song for each category: the girls' group were singing Beyoncé's, 'If I Were A Boy', the over-25s had Lady Gaga's 'Poker Face' and the groups would perform 'Nothing's Gonna Stop Us Now' by Starship.

Niall had taken his guitar with him, as had some of the other contestants. At lunchtimes they would sit outside on the steps singing together. They all loved singing so much they couldn't help themselves. One of the contestants who didn't make the live shows, John D'Ambrosio, posted some great videos of Niall playing his guitar on YouTube and other videos of him singing while someone else was playing. There are about 20 different singers joining in but you can clearly make out Zayn, Niall, Liam and Harry in different ones. They don't acknowledge each

other because only Liam and Niall had met properly when the videos were taken. If you want to see the videos you'll need to google 'John D'Ambrosio YouTube videos One Direction'.

DID YOU KNOW?

When Niall was at *X Factor* bootcamp he shared a room with Liam. Initially Liam thought that Louis was really quiet. Liam met Zayn for the first time at McDonald's, and again he thought he was quiet. Louis thought that Niall was laid-back and cheeky, and that Liam was a bit uptight and serious. The boys all think that Liam is much less serious now compared to the way he was in the beginning (he is still the most serious member of the band, though!).

Niall made it to the final day of bootcamp along with 29 other boys, but the judges could only put through eight of them to the judges' houses round. When his name wasn't called he was devastated because that meant he was going home. He was so pleased when he was told to go back on the stage with Harry, Liam, Louis and Zayn because the judges had decided that although they didn't think they were strong enough individually, they were putting them together as a group. Niall's *X Factor* journey wasn't over yet!

DID YOU KNOW?

The boys spent three weeks at Harry's house practising, and sang lots of songs by boy bands and also some solo artists' songs because they didn't know which song they were going to be asked to sing by Simon. They rehearsed songs by Robbie Williams, Coldplay and many more.

For the judges' houses round Niall and the boys flew out to Marbella, Spain and had one chance to impress their mentor, Simon Cowell. As soon as Simon heard Niall and the boys sing 'Torn' together he knew that they had huge potential and could be world class. He told an interviewer from *Rolling Stone* magazine in April 2012: 'When they came to my house in Spain and performed, after about a millionth of a second [I knew they'd be huge]. I tried to keep a straight face for a bit of drama for the show.

'I remember sitting next to this girl [Sinitta], who I was working with. The second they left, we jumped out of the chair and said, "These guys are incredible!" They just had it.'

Simon could tell that they had worked out everything themselves and they were good friends. Once he'd told them they were through to the live shows he got to know them and to find out what they're really like. He admired their drive and the fact that they weren't afraid to say what type of band they wanted to be, they didn't want to be puppets.

Niall's family and close friends knew that he had auditioned but they couldn't tell anyone how well he was doing until the *X Factor* shows were broadcast on TV in the September, so they had to wait months to find out the result. Niall didn't keep his big brother up to date at all because he was scared he'd tell people that he had made it to the live shows before the judges' houses episodes were shown on TV. If Greg had told people, it might have been leaked to the press and Niall could well have been kicked out of One Direction.

After the judges' houses episodes were broadcast, his family were free to tell anyone and everyone how proud they were of Niall. His dad Bobby told the local paper: 'He is very witty and good-humoured. He could probably do a better Geordie accent than Cheryl Cole!'

His mum Maura had supported Niall when he sang at the *Stars In Their Eyes* show, but to travel to London every week to cheer him on in the live shows was a million times better (but very scary at the same time – his family wanted him to never be in the bottom two!). Maura had never thought of Niall singing in a group before (she had always thought he would be a solo artist), but she loved Harry, Liam, Louis and Zayn when she met them.

CHAPTER 3

SINGING TO MILLIONS

Getting to perform on stage every week in front of millions of people felt incredible to Niall, because it was all he had ever dreamed about. Although he had originally wanted to be a solo artist, getting to stand next to four great friends and entertain everybody was an amazing feeling. He loved their practices all week, their rehearsals on the day and then the actual performances on the night – the only hard thing was waiting to see whether they would have to sing for survival on the Sunday night.

ONE DIRECTIONS X FACTOR JOURNEY

Week one: Number 1s – 'Viva La Vida' by Coldplay
Week two: Heroes – 'My Life Would Suck Without You' by Kelly Clarkson

Week three: Guilty Pleasures – 'Nobody Knows' by Pink
Week four: Halloween – 'Total Eclipse Of The Heart' by Bonnie Tyler
Week five: American Anthems – 'Kids In America' by Kim Wilde
Week six: Elton John – 'Something About The Way You Look Tonight'
Week seven: The Beatles – 'All You Need Is Love'
Week eight: Rock – 'Summer Of '69' by Bryan Adams and 'You Are So Beautiful' by Joe Cocker
Week nine: Semi Final – 'Only Girl In The World' by Rihanna and 'Chasing Cars' by Snow Patrol
Week 10: Final – 'Your Song' by Elton John, 'She's the One' by Robbie Williams and 'Torn' by Natalie Imbruglia

Most weeks the boys got great feedback from Simon Cowell, Louis Walsh, Dannii Minogue and Cheryl Cole, but occasionally the judges had negative things to say. This was usually because they felt that Simon, the boys' mentor, had cheated by choosing a song that didn't fit with the week's theme, or to say the staging wasn't right.

In week seven, the theme was The Beatles and the boys sang 'All You Need Is Love'. The reaction they got from the judges was mixed.

Louis Walsh said: 'Hey, One Direction, thank God for you guys! You lifted the whole energy in the studio. Good to see the Fab Five singing the Fab Four. The hysteria here has lifted your game – you are in it for the long hall, yes!'

Dannii Minogue liked their performance but didn't feel that Niall and Zayn had done very well. She said: 'Guys, another fantastic performance. I've always given you good comments, I

just have to say tonight, you guys [Niall and Zayn] were struggling. I don't know if it was caught on-camera, but you were struggling with the backing vocals. You didn't know if you were coming in or out. Don't let the other guys down – you have to work as a group.'

Cheryl Cole used her feedback to have a go at Simon, saying: 'I could get into the whole "I don't know why your mentor put you on a plain platform like that", but I won't because above everything else, that was another great performance from you guys.'

It must have been hard for Niall and the boys to hear negative comments from Dannii and to listen to Cheryl having a go at their mentor. Simon wasn't happy with his fellow judges' comments and declared: 'Who cares about the platform? Can I just say, guys: as always, you worked hard, delivered a fantastic, unique version of the song, and please, for anyone at home who saw what happened last week (Aiden Grimshaw, one of the favourites, had been sent home), please don't think these guys are safe. This lot [Louis, Dannii and Cheryl] do not want you to do well in the competition. *I* do... please vote!'

Cheryl's comment about the platform One Direction were standing on came because Simon had criticised her decision to place her act – Cher Lloyd – on a staircase for her performance of 'Imagine' earlier in the night.

Afterwards Niall and the boys were interviewed in front of the backstage cameras but they were not too concerned about Dannii suggesting that Niall and Zayn didn't do well – in fact Niall thought it was their strongest performance yet. Liam shrugged off the comments, saying, 'Dannii gave us a bad comment, but we're going to get bad comments so we've just got to take it on board and improve it next week.'

As One Direction sailed through each week Niall acquired

more and more fans — and the whole of Ireland was behind him. His hometown Mullingar decided to put huge 'Niall Horan One Direction' signs on their recycling bin wagons to show how much they were backing One Direction to win and local shopkeepers put up signs in their windows too.

When One Direction made the live shows Niall's school posted a message on their website saying they'd be supporting him 100 per cent. One of his closest friends from school — Graham Dowling — told the *Herald* newspaper: 'He's like a celebrity here, there are posters everywhere.' Graham is the brother of Kieron, who used to support Niall in his talent shows. He'd known him since they were five or six years old and said he was a born pop star.

DID YOU KNOW?

Graham is a talented singer, too, and in 2012 he appeared in the first series of *The Voice Ireland*. Niall tried to encourage Directioners to vote for him, tweeting: 'Irish directioners! one of my best mates my whole life, we live next door, went to school together. Graham Dowling from the voice!' and 'the live shows start this week and we need to make sure we vote for him! he is a legend.'

Sadly Graham didn't win, but he still did really well and he is so thankful for the support Niall gave him, tweeting '@NiallOfficial Nialler man cheers for the SHOUTOUT!'

Niall's school friends and teachers voted for him every week. They were asked to give interviews to their local press, which encouraged more people to vote. His close friend Adam Keena admitted to the *Belfast Telegraph*: 'Not many people from a small town like Mullingar believe that they can actually become

something but Niall has actually changed everyone's perspective on that. He has inspired us all to believe that we can make something of ourselves if we try hard enough.'

His principal Joe O'Meara added: 'He is such an exceptional lad. He has found his niche big time and he is on top of the world. He's a lovely, unassuming guy and very well mannered. When he got the X Factor he came in to ask me could he postpone his Leaving Cert and he is welcome back at any time. We'd love to have him back.'

Niall's local fans were looking forward to seeing him and the rest of the One Direction lads switch on their town's Christmas lights, but they were left disappointed when the boys had to cancel. They were too busy rehearsing their two songs for Rock week and couldn't afford to fly out to Ireland as they would have risked being unprepared for the show on the following Saturday. Niall's dad was devastated when he heard they wouldn't be flying over as he had been telling his customers they would be there. Bobby told the Herald at the time: 'Everyone is very interested in them, there has been great support.'

Niall, Maura, Greg and the wider family felt like they were dreaming. Bobby summed it up: 'It's surreal when you see it, we're just ordinary people. It's like doing the Lotto – you don't expect to win it and he didn't expect to go so far, but they're still there!'

DID YOU KNOW?

Niall's got a stepdad called Chris. Maura and Chris got married in 2005 and they love in Edgeworthstown, County Longford.

During the 10 weeks of X Factor live shows Shows Niall got to

meet some of his favourite artists who were performing on the Sunday Night results show. He is a huge Michael Bublé fan and says he wouldn't have taken up singing if it wasn't for Frank Sinatra and Michael Bublé. Naturally, meeting Michael Bublé in week three was a huge deal for him.

In the week leading up to the *X Factor* final, his family were interviewed by the *Belfast Telegraph* and did what they could to encourage people to pick up their phones and vote for Niall and the boys to win. They were up against Cher Lloyd, Rebecca Ferguson and Matt Cardle. Niall's dad Bobby said, 'I am so proud of him. I would love to see him win it.

'I think Irish votes could be the difference between One Direction winning and not winning the show – it could hang on getting Mary Byrne's Irish voters on board.'

Mary from Ballyfermot, Dublin had been the contestant voted off in the semi-final and she really wanted Niall, Harry, Zayn, Louis and Liam to win. During a radio interview she asked her fans to vote for One Direction in the final.

Niall's mum, Maura, echoed his dad when she said: 'It would be the biggest dream ever for Niall to win *The X Factor*. They are winners for even getting into the final, but I know in their little hearts that they will be disappointed if they don't.'

His brother Greg added: 'I'm excited but nervous for him. He has inspired me but I'm too old for my dream to be a footballer. My dream now is to see him have his dream.'

In the days leading up to the final, Niall and the boys had received good luck messages from Max George from The Wanted and singer Diana Vickers. Former *X Factor* winners Alexandra Burke and Joe McElderry both thought that One Direction had what it takes to win. One Direction had had a crazy few days: they'd enjoyed a Christmas meal in the *X Factor* house with the rest of the finalists, put in extra rehearsals to

perfect all three songs they would be singing (and the winners' song) and spent a day travelling all over England, visiting their hometowns. They couldn't fly over to Ireland because of heavy snow, so they did a live link-up with Ireland FM instead from Granada Studios. Ireland FM has a huge breakfast show and so thousands of people heard their interview.

The first hometown they visited was Doncaster in south Yorkshire, where Louis is from. They went to Hall Cross School and the students went crazy the second they saw Louis and the boys. There were hundreds of people there to cheer them on in the playground and once inside the school hall they got so much applause. Louis was blown away by their reaction and said that he found being on his school's stage more nerve-wracking than appearing on the *X Factor* stage on a Saturday night!

The second hometown they visited was Harry's – Holmes Chapel in Cheshire. People had made their own banners with 'good luck' messages on them and a mini-party was held in Harry's house. They couldn't spend long there because there were hundreds of fans waiting for them at a music store in Birmingham in the West Midlands: Zayn's home city. When their car drove up, Zayn couldn't believe how many people were there to support them. He had visited the music store many times but no one had so much as batted an eyelid before. The boys imagined what it would be like to one day visit when their own CDs were on sale in the store and Zayn imagined doing a signing there. Louis told *X Factor* cameras at the time: 'It was like nothing we'd ever seen before.'

The boys might have been tired but they had one more stop to make before they made their way back to London. They had a performance to do in front of thousands of screaming girls in Wolverhampton in the west Midlands, Liam's home city. Their

X Factor mentor Simon Cowell joined them and they had a blast. Liam told *X Factor* cameras in the band's last-ever video diary for the show: 'Wolverhampton was absolutely awesome, the crowd were absolutely amazing! Five thousand people there waiting for us and we went on stage and did three songs and it was the best gig any of us had ever done.'

Harry commented: 'It's really exciting for us to think we're going to be doing loads of little gigs like that and some to bigger crowds than that.'

And Liam summed up how they were all feeling: 'We just really want to thank everybody for all the support we've had so far throughout the competition and we just can't believe it, it's unreal. Thank you so much to everybody who's been voting for us and please keep voting.'

The boys did so well visiting four out of their five hometowns when they could have just chosen one or two. Rebecca Ferguson only had to visit Liverpool, Merseyside, Matt Cardle visited Colne Engaine near Colchester in Essex, while Cher Lloyd only had to travel to Malvern in Worcestershire. But Niall and the boys didn't want to let their home fans down and if it hadn't been for the heavy snow, they would have flown to Ireland and visited five out of the five.

The final was taking place over two nights: on the Saturday one act would be sent home, and then on the Sunday the act coming third would be sent home before the final two battled it out to become *The X Factor* winner 2010. On the night of the final the whole town of Mullingar was ready to party. Brian Smith, who runs the Greville Arms Hotel in Mullingar, told the *Belfast Telegraph* he was putting on a big *X Factor* party, saying: 'It will be a huge bash. The town is just buzzing.' There was also a big party at the Bed nightclub, which is where Niall's cousins decided to watch the show. Robert Horan told journalists that

they were 'very, very nervous'. Here's a rundown of who sang what on the night.

Saturday night, song number one:
One Direction – 'Your Song' by Elton John
Matt Cardle – 'Here With Me' by Dido
Rebecca Ferguson – 'Like A Star' by Corinne Bailey Rae
Cher Lloyd – Mash-up of '369' by Cupid ft. B.o.B. and 'Get Ur Freak On' by Missy Elliott

The judges all had different views about everyone's performances, including One Direction. Louis Walsh said: 'Hey, One Direction, you're in the final, I hope you're here tomorrow night! It's amazing how five guys have gelled so well. I know you're all best friends. I've never seen a band cause so much hysteria so early in their career. I definitely think that you've got an amazing future. Niall, everybody in Ireland must vote for Niall, yes!'

Dannii Minogue reacted by saying: 'Guys, you have worked so hard in this competition. You were thrown together, you deserve to be here and I'd love to see you in the final tomorrow.'

Cheryl Cole said: 'You know what, I have thoroughly enjoyed watching you guys growing every week, having the most amount of fun possible and I think that you deserve to be standing on that stage tomorrow night.'

Simon Cowell lavished One Direction with praise: 'I just would like to say after hearing the first two performances tonight, Matt and Rebecca, they were so good my heart was sinking. And then you came up onstage, you've got to remember that you're 16/17 years old, and each of you proved that you should be there as individual singers, you gave it 1,000

per cent. It's been an absolute pleasure working with you. I really hope people bother to pick up the phone, put you through to tomorrow because you deserve to be there.'

Then the boys had to go through it all again and perform their second song of the night.

Saturday night, song two – the duets:
One Direction – 'She's The One' with Robbie Williams
Matt Cardle – 'Unfaithful' with Rihanna
Rebecca Ferguson – 'Beautiful' with Christina Aguilera
Cher Lloyd – Mash-up of 'Where Is The Love' and 'I Gotta Feeling' with will.i.am

The boys had been so excited when they found out that they would be singing with the legendary Robbie Williams, who had been in one of their favourite boy bands, Take That. It was an unbelievable opportunity and they didn't want to mess up (Harry and Louis in particular were huge fans). They all wore brightly coloured suits and as the music started there was just the five of them lined up: Liam first, then Niall, Harry in the middle, then Louis, with Zayn at the end. They started to sing and then Louis said: 'Right, there's a man who is a hero to all of us, here he is... the incredible... Robbie Williams!'

Robbie appeared from behind them and joined the line. Niall looked so chuffed and the five of them moved in closer. Niall and Liam put their arms around each other – loving the moment they were singing with Robbie Williams! Robbie gave them each a high-five as they carried on singing, finishing the song as a six-piece. They got in a huddle and gave each other a hug before Robbie picked up Niall from the ground. Niall looked so happy.

Robbie told *X Factor* host Dermot O'Leary that he understood how the boys must be feeling at the start of their journey before adding that he thought they rocked. Harry was so grateful, telling Dermot: 'It's just incredible, it's such an honour to sing with Robbie.'

Their mentor Simon added: 'Robbie is a great friend to the show – very, very generous with his time and he's made these boys the night of their lives. Thank you, Robbie.'

After everyone had performed it was time to reveal the results. It was so tense as the four acts waited on the stage to see if they had done enough to go through to Sunday's show. The first name to be called out was Rebecca: she was the first act safe. Next was One Direction – they were safe. They jumped up and down and hugged Simon, they were so happy. The final act safe was Matt, meaning that Cher had to leave the competition.

The boys must have struggled to get to sleep that night; they wanted so badly to win. Sunday, the final, was just around the corner.

Sunday night, the final song:
One Direction – 'Torn' by Natalie Imbruglia
Matt Cardle – 'Firework' by Katy Perry
Rebecca Ferguson – 'Sweet Dreams' by Eurythmics

Just as on Saturday night, the judges each had different comments to give the final contestants. Louis Walsh said: 'One Direction, you're in the final, you could be the first band to win *The X Factor* – it's up to the public at home. But you've got brilliant chemistry. I love the harmonies. I love the song choice and we've got five new pop stars!'

Dannii Minogue said: 'Guys, you've done all the right things

to make your place here in the final. That was a fantastic performance! Whatever happens tonight I'm sure you guys are going to go on and release records and be the next big band.'

Cheryl Cole remarked: 'It's been so lovely to watch you guys from your first audition. To think that was only a few months ago. I really believe that you've got a massive future ahead of you and I wanna say thank you for being such lovely guys to be around. It's been great getting to know you and good luck with the show tonight.'

Simon Cowell beamed: 'Let's be clear, anyone who comes into this final has got a great chance of bettering their future but this is a competition and in terms of the competition, in terms of who's worked the hardest, who I think deserves to win based on the future of something we haven't seen before, I would love to hear your names read out at the end of the competition. Because I think you deserve it.'

After all the contestants had performed, the results were in! Waiting for the results had been intense the night before, but nothing compared to how Niall and the boys were feeling on the final show. When Dermot announced that the first act through was Matt they must have been gutted. They were up against Rebecca, and she had an amazing voice. It seemed to take Dermot ages to reveal the next act through and it wasn't Niall and the boys – it was Rebecca. Simon turned his back straight away, as if to hide his shock, and the boys all looked devastated. They congratulated Rebecca but it was so hard; they had to hold back the tears as they were shown their best bits and asked by Dermot what the highlights had been for them.

Louis said: 'It's been absolutely incredible. For me the highlight when we first sang together at judges' houses, that was unbelievable and you know want, we've done our absolute best, we've worked hard.'

Zayn added: 'We're definitely going to stay together, this isn't the last of One Direction!'

Hundreds of Niall's biggest supporters in Mullingar had turned up at special parties to watch him win, so when Dermot announced that the act in third place was One Direction they were gutted, shouting out 'Oh no!' at the big screens. Niall's cousin Aoife told the *Independent.ie* that Niall and the boys had still given Mullingar the 'feel-good' factor. He might not have won but they were all so proud of him. To see someone from their town singing alongside Robbie Williams was unbelievable.

The boys then had to leave the stage, as Matt and Rebecca had to sing the song they would release if they won. When Dermot announced that Matt was the winner the band was so happy because he had become a good mate. They had said from the beginning that if they didn't win the show then they would like it to be Matt. As he sang the winner's song, all of the *X Factor* live show acts ran on stage and mobbed him. One Direction were the first to get to him; Harry joined in with the singing and Niall encouraged the audience to cheer even more for Matt. He also grabbed Matt's first CD and gave it a kiss.

After the show finished, they tweeted: 'Congratulations Matt! Please support Matt by buying When We Collide iTunes…'

Niall and the boys were summoned to Simon's dressing room, which was a bit scary for them. Only the winner had a guaranteed record deal so they didn't know what was going to happen. Niall, Harry, Zayn, Liam and Louis really hoped that Simon would sign them to his own record label, but they couldn't be sure because they'd only managed to come third. He didn't tell them the good news straight away but eventually he did – he was going to make their dreams come true; they were going to be recording artists!

They couldn't tell anyone because it was Matt's night and nothing had been signed, so they had to try and keep it a secret. Simon didn't want the press to find out until they were ready to make an official announcement. Niall and the boys had to go to the *X Factor* wrap party the next night as if nothing had happened. It must have been so hard for Niall not being able to tell his friends, but he could at least tell his mum and dad. Unfortunately, the press somehow found out and it was huge news, but no one knew who had leaked the story. Some people didn't feel that the boys should have been given a record deal so soon because they believed it made a mockery of the show as the winner was supposed to be the one who landed the deal.

DID YOU KNOW?

One Direction had a meeting with their management company the morning after the wrap party, so they had to be up before 6am!

In the days that followed the final, the boys had lots of interviews to do and they were asked loads of questions about their time on *X Factor*. Harry told *Digital Spy* what his highlight was: 'When we walked in and saw the studio for the first time. Then when us five stood behind the doors for the first time on the live show, for that first song – for me that was the best moment. That was where we were actually doing it, the real thing, for the first time. That was a big moment!'

For Niall, getting to the final was a big moment, and something he will never forget. For a while, he didn't have time to let it sink in as they had appearances to make, performances to do, and they also had their first management meetings with their new record label. And he couldn't go home to Ireland because the band had had to move into a smart London hotel

the day after *X Factor* finished until their record company found them a suitable apartment to live in.

For Niall being on *The Late Late Show* in Ireland a few months later was a big moment for him because he used to watch it on a Friday night before he became part of One Direction. His whole family were excited and even his mum and granny came along and sat in the green room! The other lads love Niall's granny because she is very, very small and very funny.

Niall told the host, Ryan Tubridy, of *The Late Late Show* in Ireland that the move to London was a bit daunting but he liked it. 'We all live in the same complex, we go to work, come back, sleep and eat,' he said. Irish singer Niall Breslin (known as 'Bressie') lives close to Niall and the two are good mates.

CHAPTER 4

GIRLS

When Niall was on *The X Factor* he admitted in a backstage video that he had kissed 20 girls. One of the vocal coaches witnessed him flirting with Cheryl Cole and told *Buzz* magazine: 'Louis and Niall from the band were sort of chatting Cheryl up the other night, and she started teasing them, asking if they would like her as a mentor instead of Simon. She understands best why they would be attractive to teenage girls, and is always flirting with them because she sees what the young girls see in them.'

One of Niall's housemates (and rivals) during *The X Factor* was Amelia Lily. They were photographed leaving the studio together, which made people speculate that something might be going on between them. It wasn't – they did swap numbers but Amelia prefers boys with dark hair and neither of them was

looking for romance anyway; they were concentrating on their music and on getting as far in the competition as possible. The press also tried to suggest that Niall fancied Rebecca Creighton from the girl group Belle Amie, with Rebecca's sister telling *OK!* magazine: 'Rebecca and Niall Horan are both from Ireland, so they've been coming home together and they've really bonded.

'He even came to her 21st birthday party. They met on *X Factor* but have been good friends since then, and both the families have met each other.'

Niall was also linked to the other girls in the group by the press. Like One Direction, the Belle Amie girls – Sophia Wardman, Esther Campbell, Geneva Lane and Rebecca Creighton – had been put together by the judges at bootcamp. They lasted in the competition until week four. The girls really wanted people to like them but felt that being a girl group held them back.

Sophia from the group told Viking FM: 'I think it's a lot easier for the boys to do well because they're five cute boys and the girls are always going to love them and they are really good. I think for us, we just wanted a little bit more help – just because it's harder for us to get people to like us, to get the right song and the right styling.

'You could put the boys out there in bin bags and sing "Baa Baa Black Sheep" and they'd go through with flying colours. I think it's just a lot easier for them than us.'

Niall and the boys did have a slightly easier ride because they were a boy band, but they still had to put in the hours. Also, it was harder for them in some ways because they had five people singing rather than four.

> **DID YOU KNOW?**
> The girl group Little Mix won *The X Factor* the following year, so *they* obviously didn't have problems getting people to like them!

When they were living in the *X Factor* house together the press suggested that something might be going on between Niall and Sophia, even though there was quite a big age gap. It was said they'd been hugging each other a lot and had kissed on the lips. Sophia set the record straight in a video diary for the official *X Factor* website. She said: 'I can honestly, openly say that there is nothing going on between me and Niall. Niall is like a little ba-ba to me. He is seven years younger than me, and that would just be weird! As cute as he is, he is still all yours, girls, so don't you worry!

'They are good to have fun with and they always want hugs, but they are literally like our little brothers.'

Geneva added: 'Just like what Sophia said, they're like our little buddies – there's honestly nothing going on. We're focused on the prize. There is honestly nothing going on, they are all yours!'

The boys sometimes treated the girls like annoying big sisters and thought they were always moaning. The girls' room was directly underneath theirs so they would stomp around and try and make as much noise as possible when the girls were trying to sleep, just to irritate them. They would also sneak into their room to steal their bras and run around the house with them on their heads.

> **DID YOU KNOW?**
> Niall's first kiss was with a French foreign exchange student when he was 11. He was very nervous and can't really remember what it was like, or remember the girl.

She was staying at his friend's house. Back then his celebrity crush was Jennifer Lopez because she was very popular at the time and she had a nice bum. He didn't date the girl he kissed because she had to go back to France, but two years later he had his first girlfriend.

DID YOU KNOW?

Niall's celebrity crush is Demi Lovato, for Liam it's Leona Lewis; Louis also likes Demi Lovato (but he said it as a joke to Niall), and Harry and Zayn like Rihanna.

Niall was going out with Holly Scally before he was on *X Factor* but he decided to end things so that he could concentrate on his music. He thinks she is an amazing person and they are still friends. Holly is two years younger than Niall and they met when she was 13 at a school disco. They dated for nine months. Sometimes on their dates Niall would sing songs to her and one day they went to a lake and he hired a boat. Other times they saved their money and just chatted or bought chips from a café. They used to call each other 'babe'.

Niall was very apologetic when he told Holly they should split over the phone. Holly explained to *Now* magazine how it happened. She revealed: 'One day Niall called and said, "I think we should finish because I never see you."

'I said, "Yeah, I know. I understand. So it's cool."

'I think he felt bad because he kept saying, "I'm so sorry". I tried to sound like it was no big deal but it was a bit sad for me.'

Niall's mum Maura liked Holly but understood why the relationship ended. She told the *Herald*: 'He had a girlfriend at

34

home, from his school days, before he auditioned for *X Factor*. But then he was doing that and she was doing exams, so life is very different for him now. I don't know if he sees much of her when he's home; she was lovely, but they were only 16 at the time – there's never anything too steady about a relationship at that age.'

Poor Holly has had lots of abuse on Twitter and one obsessive fan decided to spread a rumour that she had died. They posted up a photo of her with the message 'RIP Holly' and said she had had cancer and had died, tweeting: 'Guys, I had some really bad news, Niall's ex-girlfriend Holly has passed away due to cancer.'

Holly was understandably upset and angry when she found out what had been said, and that so many people believed she had died. She admitted to *Now* magazine, 'Hearing that RIP Holly Scally was trending was terrifying.'

She had retaliated by sending some tweets herself, which contained the f-word. Because of this she received even more negative messages. 'I was so furious that I hit back and said that my new boyfriend was "better than Niall f**king Horan",' she continued. 'In Mullingar using the f-word is so common it was meant as a joke. But when a newspaper ran the story, the hate escalated and one girl tweeted that I should kill myself.'

Holly isn't the only girl connected to the boys to receive hate messages. Louis' girlfriend, Eleanor Calder, has suffered lots of abuse from jealous fans. Louis thinks it's disgusting and once tweeted: 'Truth of the matter is it's actually not funny in the slightest. I'm reading through some horrible tweets very p*ssed off!'

Sometimes parents can reveal a bit too much in interviews – and this was certainly the case when Niall's dad Bobby was

interviewed by *Heat* magazine in May 2012. He said: 'There's a local girl that Niall loves. I know he thinks of her as his sweetheart. She's very attractive and they're close, but I don't know whether he's made any advances on her yet. She would stand her ground with any of these beautiful celebrities. She's a brunette with big brown eyes and pale skin like Niall's. She's from the town, but the other end to us and I always knew Niall has big feelings for her.'

Bobby also revealed that Niall had never really brought girls he was dating home but he did have female friends and they would sit and chat on the wall outside their house.

The press have tried to suggest that Niall and American *X Factor* judge Demi Lovato are dating but this isn't the case. When asked whether they were in a promotion video for the *X Factor* she said: 'No, I'm not. He's really sweet and he's one of my really good friends now but I'm single at the moment and I plan to be for a long time because I need to focus on my career and myself and my wellbeing before I think about getting in a relationship with anyone.'

DID YOU KNOW?

In the first song One Direction released, 'What Makes You Beautiful', the boys sing about not needing makeup to cover up – just being the way you are is enough for them. Niall, in particular, believes this and when a fan tweeted: 'Don't need make up, to cover up... NEXT JOKE PLEASE BOYS,' he decided he needed to reply. He tweeted: 'Well I like a girl who don't wear make-up [sic].' Over 14,000 fans re-tweeted his message.

Niall hasn't had lots of girlfriends so when discussing relationships with *OK!* magazine he said: 'I've not actually been

on too many dates. I just like sitting at home, chilling and watching a movie.' He thinks he understands girls more than Harry, Zayn, Louis and Liam, telling the magazine: 'I'm an emotional guy, so I don't have to worry about that.'

A fan once asked Niall if he would ever date ugly girls. 'I can't date someone who doesn't exist,' he replied. Niall doesn't care about looks; he cares about a girl's personality and what she is like. He believes that when he falls in love it will be because of how he feels about a girl in his heart, not because of what she looks like.

DID YOU KNOW?

Niall isn't a guy who spends hours in the gym. He told fans: 'I don't have biceps, I just flex my eyebrows.'

Niall and Harry really fancy the Kardashian sisters and when they were on an American radio show, Harry decided to hold up a photo of Kim Kardashian with a post-it note stuck on it, saying: 'Call Me, maybe? ;)'.

DID YOU KNOW?

Before Harry started dating Caroline Flack, he held up a sign during an interview, saying 'Flackster! Never too old. Let's make it happen!! Lots of love, Harry S'.

Niall tweeted Kim's sister Khloe and her husband Lamar Odom, saying: 'Hey khloe, we are coming to dallas next week for a fan event performing and stuff ! you and lemar [sic] should come along!' She replied: 'We would love to!! When and where?! LOL depending on if there's a game we would love to come.'

Afterwards she tweeted: 'Ugh! Lamar will be playing out of

town in Houston& I will be in LA but I come back that day. Keep me posted on the time wooo.'

Niall will have girlfriends in the future but for now he is focusing on his music.

CHAPTER 5

FAMILY

Now that Niall's base is in London his family don't get to see him as much as they would like. He only spent 30 days in Ireland in 2011 because he was so busy working on the band's first album and promoting it.

When Niall gets time off to go home he doesn't plan loads of nights out; he likes chilling out with his family and being the old Niall. They just stay in most of the time and he invites his friends round for a couple of drinks. His dad Bobby told the *Mirror*: 'He's through the door and straight to his room and when we do talk, he does it while he's strumming his guitar, and you have to talk to him over the chords. It's very funny but that's the way he is. He's not a big drinker but we often go for a pint when he's home. He's got very good friends here... he even flew one of them, Sean Cullen, out to America. They grew up together.'

Niall loves spending time with Sean and they checked out New York's tourist sites, posing for photos at the top of the Empire State Building. Afterwards Niall tweeted one photo to his followers and wrote: 'Unreal day out, here's me and @seancullen95 on the top of the empire state building' and 'Last day off, last time I'll see the fam for a while and @seancullen95 so gona chill out.'

DID YOU KNOW?

If Niall had to pick a fictional best friend he would choose Homer Simpson.

People in Mullingar now recognise Bobby and Greg, Niall's big brother. Greg was invited to judge a talent competition at Clarke's Bar in August 2012. *Clarke's Got Talent* was a fundraiser for Mullingar Town Football Club and as well as Greg, Niall's friend Graham Dowling (from *The Voice*) was judging and singing.

DID YOU KNOW?

Niall still gets starstruck and whenever he meets someone famous he will ring Greg to tell him. No matter what happens in the future Niall and Greg will always be really close friends as well as brothers.

On his dad's birthday Niall tweeted: 'Happy birthday, best father on the planet! Bobby horan, hero!' He also tweeted a special message to his nan on 24 August, writing: 'Happy birthday to my nanny! Maggie nolan! Unreal at making dinner! #happybirthdaymaggie.'

DID YOU KNOW?

When the boys were asked by an interviewer to think of a girl who doesn't know she's beautiful they struggled — because they kept thinking of famous people — but then said that Niall's nan was a girl who didn't know how beautiful she was.

Niall was devastated in August 2012 when one of his friends from Mullingar was killed in a car crash. Two other men were injured, so Niall asked fans on Twitter to '#PrayForMullingarBoys'. Sadly, one of the men died a few days later. Niall told fans on Twitter that his friend Quentin will be missed and that he was thinking of the Reilly family.

DID YOU KNOW?

Niall's brother Greg joked in one interview that Niall is no longer the most famous person in Mullingar. For the 2012 London Olympics, a show jumper called Josh Murphy and a boxer (John Joe Nevin) were competing. John Joe came away with a silver medal, and the whole of Mullingar were so proud. Niall tweeted: 'On the phone to @johnJoeNevin for the last hour! He's a sound lad! We grew up 100 yards away from each other, now he's goin for an olympic medal.'

When John Joe was in the quarter-final against Mexico's Oscar Valdez Fierro Niall really wanted to be there to watch, so he tweeted: 'Really wana [sic] go watch @johnJoeNevin tonight! Cant get tickets anywhere' and 'Never wanted tickets for somethin more in my life than i do now!'

A few hours later he tweeted: 'I made it to the fight in the

end! Cannot believe im here to watch this happen! Me and @williedevine ran 1.5 lkm to the excel and made it.'

Niall posted up a photo of himself and his friend Willie in the arena, with the different international flags in the background, and tweeted: 'Meself and @williedevine at the boxing! #mullingarboysdontstop.'

They were both thrilled when John Joe won 19-13.

The night before John Joe's final, Harry was going to the party of his friend Nick Grimshaw but Niall decided to go to the Funky Buddha nightclub with Josh Devine, who plays drums for One Direction, and Joey Cottle, who has played keyboard for them. After getting home, Niall tweeted: 'Great time at @JoshDevineDrums and @JoeyCottle's birthday party! Home now! Bedtime, set for the final tomorrow! Cmon @johnJoeNevin! Hero.' Niall wanted to share with his fans how much he was looking forward to watching the Olympics final with John Joe Nevin taking on Great Britain's Luke Campbell.

Sadly, John Joe didn't get the gold but he did win the silver medal and Niall celebrated with him. To see the photo of Niall with John Joe, go to his friend Willie's Twitter page: @williedevine.

In the weeks leading up to the Closing Ceremony whenever they got a free moment the boys had loved watching the athletes compete and Niall in particular wished he had been able to compete in an event.

Niall's best Olympics tweets:

'Do they have an egg and spoon race in the olympics! I wana try! Always did well at sports day!!'

'Gettin up early this mornin just t watch the Olympics, with a cup of tea! #YOP.'

'Love the Olympics coz it brings all countries together! all the different countries flags together in the crowd.'

'All the Irish athletes competing at #london2012, good luck to all of u! As usual your country is standing right behind you!'

'What's with all the empty seats at the Olympics if they wan a give any tickets away i'll have them hahaha!'

'Went t bed like an hour ago and wanted t get a super early night! But i cant stop watchin #London2012 its crazy! USA v Argentina #Bball.'

'Met soo many incredible people today! The who, brian may, spice girls, take that! liam gallagher, just a day none of us will ever forget.'

CHAPTER 6

FAN LOVE

On 25 November 2011, Harry was the first member of One Direction to have a million followers on Twitter. Then on 22 December 2011 One Direction fans decided to help Niall to gain more followers as he had the least number of all the boys. They wanted to help him get 900,000 followers, so at 2pm they tweeted #followNiallOfficial and it was soon trending. At the time they had no idea that by April 2012 he would have three million. Niall was so happy that he tweeted: 'Wow! 3million followers, thank you soo much! #directionersareincredible.' By October 2012 he would have over six million and he's been gaining more and more fans every day. Niall is by far the most popular member of One Direction in America. He has the second most number of followers on Twitter now, and could soon overtake Harry.

Maura brought Niall up to respect girls and told him to smile and pose for photos with fans – not that he needs telling, anyway. He's not at all big headed and likes to take time out to thank the people who buy One Direction's records and vote for them to win big awards.

DID YOU KNOW?

Niall thinks the biggest turn-off in a girl is if she is 'too in your face', thinking she is so hot. For Harry, the biggest turn-off is spitting.

Niall's family have got used to One Direction fans turning up to see if he is home so they can try and get an autograph or photo. They even turn up when he's not there. His dad Bobby has met fans from Canada and America who have flown over to Ireland especially. He let one mum and daughter have a quick peek in Niall's room because they had travelled so far – but don't expect the same if you turn up on his doorstep. Niall's fans are always polite and don't get aggressive if Bobby says they can't come in. Like Harry's mum Anne, Bobby gets a lot of fan mail for his son and sorts through it. Fans are supposed to send it to their official fan-mail address but sometimes they come direct.

DID YOU KNOW?

Sometimes fans will post bras that they want Niall to autograph. Handing them over can be an odd experience for Bobby. Niall is given so many gifts that he can't possibly keep them all so he puts them in boxes, which go to hospitals. The patients must be thrilled when they are given the toys, flags and other gifts!

One Direction have thousands of fans but Niall would like even more. He explained to Tumblr's *Storyboard blog* in July 2012: 'We want to see more boy fans, as seeing them in the crowd is cool, it's 90 per cent girls, but we want to expand our fan base. We want all people to like us.'

Niall, Zayn, Liam, Louis and Harry are very grateful to every single fan that supports them, as Liam explained in the same interview: 'It's very flattering obviously as we can see how much they care for us. We just hope they're crying tears of joy! None of us could obviously ever have imagined this just two years ago. I don't think anyone could have seen this coming, to be honest.'

All of One Direction are determined not to let their fans down and to create great music that they will enjoy. After all, they are doing what they used to dream about before they were famous. Being famous does have its drawbacks, though: they are followed by the paparazzi wherever they go and sometimes Niall gets scared by the hundreds of fans who turn up outside studios and venues to see him. His dad revealed all to the *Mirror*: 'There are hordes of young girls around him, and not much room to breathe anywhere. He says it can be frightening. Coming out of airports and girls crowding around their cars, he's started to get really claustrophobic.'

Sometimes fans can faint or burst into tears because they are so excited to see Niall. Niall thinks it might happen because there aren't many concerts to go to in some of the countries they visit and the girls get so excited because they are at last going to see their favourite band perform. He's amazed how long some of them will wait outside venues in the hope that they can see him, Harry, Liam, Louis and Zayn for just a few seconds and maybe get an autograph. He recommends fans bring blankets, lots of layers and plenty of

food and drink if they want to do that – he doesn't want anyone getting ill.

Harry and Zayn bought luxury cars as soon as they could but Niall wasn't in any rush to get a car, or even pass his test. He has been brought up to be careful around money and isn't about to waste it on extravagant things.

DID YOU KNOW?

Niall did buy his mum a lovely car, though, as a Christmas present!

His brother Greg admitted in July 2012 that Niall was in the process of getting a driver's licence and could buy a Range Rover in the future. Unlike Harry, Louis and Zayn, at that time he hadn't found a house that he wanted to buy, and still enjoyed staying in the apartment that his record company pays for. He's someone who likes to take his time and weigh up all the options open to him.

DID YOU KNOW?

When the boys were in New Zealand a radio producer experienced what life is like for Niall, Harry, Zayn, Liam and Louis. Guy Parsons pretended to be them by wearing a beanie hat, a scarf and some sunglasses, and managed to trick thousands of fans that had turned up to meet the band at a hotel. They followed him and it wasn't until he turned around that they realised it wasn't Niall or one of the others. Some fans decided to get their photos taken with Guy anyway. He confessed to the *Sunday Star Times*: 'I said, "I've got you, I'm not one of them." I don't think I could do that every day, but for the three minutes I was posing and running away from the girls I liked the attention.'

Niall likes sending messages to his friends from Mullingar on Twitter and when it was one of his friend's birthdays he tweeted: 'Happy birthday to one of my best mates! Brad.' Thousands of Niall's followers re-tweeted the message. When he can, he tweets messages to fans celebrating their birthdays but of course he can't tweet everyone as he gets hundreds of messages every day.

CHAPTER 7

UP ALL
NIGHT

Niall was so excited when *Up All Night* was released in Ireland on 18 November 2011. It meant the world to him that his family and friends could walk into any music store and buy an album he had recorded with four of his closest friends. He would have been happy if it charted in the top five but it charted at number one – an amazing achievement for five teenage lads. It was number two in the UK and did even better when released worldwide in 2012. Following this, it was number one in the USA, Sweden, New Zealand, Mexico, Italy, Croatia, Canada and Australia.

The first single One Direction released was 'What Makes You Beautiful' and it was number one in Ireland, Mexico and the UK and US as well as charting high in other countries.

Up All Night track list:
1. 'What Makes You Beautiful'
2. 'Gotta Be You'
3. 'One Thing'
4. 'More Than This'
5. 'Up All Night'
6. 'I Wish'
7. 'Tell Me a Lie'
8. 'Taken'
9. 'I Want'
10. 'Everything About You'
11. 'Save You Tonight'
12. 'Stole My Heart'

Limited edition – Yearbook
13. 'Stand Up'
14. 'Moments'

The seventh track on the album was 'Tell Me a Lie' and the boys were very privileged to record it because Kelly Clarkson who wrote the track doesn't usually allow other artists to have her songs. She told the *Daily Star*: 'Giving away my songs is not something I do lightly. I'm very particular about that because my songs are like my babies. If I wanted it done I can sing it myself. I'm such a writer's snob.'

Kelly isn't afraid to say no to artists if she doesn't like the way they sing, so when Simon Cowell first approached her to ask if Niall and the boys could sing one of her songs she didn't say yes straight away. 'When Simon Cowell put me forward to write for One Direction I said, "Let me hear them first",' she explained. 'Simon has been really supportive since I won *American Idol*.

'"Tell Me a Lie" is the cut I've got on 1D's album as I like the story of them, how they came together as a group. While I wrote the song for me, it didn't fit in the current album as I never want an album to sound like one thought.'

Kelly thinks that Niall and the boys come across as somewhat innocent and that's why people on both sides of the Atlantic like them. She also thinks that 'people love a story'.

For Niall, getting to number one in America was beyond his wildest dreams and he will never forget what he was doing when he found out. He told CKO196.9 Radio: 'I was in the back of a cab and I was going to Sony Music to collect my tickets; I was going to a basketball game and I was with my friend, and my manager called me up and told me we were number one. And I went crazy! I screamed my head off and the taxi driver nearly kicked me out of the car – he was freaked out.'

When Niall's dad found out that *Up All Night* was number one in America he was just starting work. Niall might be a millionaire but Bobby still works as a butcher in his local Tesco supermarket; he would never live off his son's money. Bobby is really glad One Direction have been so successful. He told the *Mirror*: 'Obviously he didn't get any school qualifications because of *The X Factor* but he's a very intelligent boy.

DID YOU KNOW?

One Direction are the second most powerful young music stars in the world. *Billboard*'s 21 under 21 list saw Justin Bieber as the most powerful. Their former *X Factor* friend Cher Lloyd was number eight in the list. Niall sent her a message in May 2012 to try and arrange a meet-up. He said: '@CherLloyd cher bear!how are ya? hows things in the states?we might cross paths at some stage soon. gotta meet up. here with @savan_kotecha.'

Before 'What Makes You Beautiful' was released McFly gave an interview in which they admitted that they wished they had recorded it instead. Drummer Harry Judd told the *Daily Star*: 'They're young, like when we started, so it makes me feel old. But it's a compliment to us if people think they sound like early McFly. I wish we had their new single for ourselves – it's fresh.'

Lead singer Tom Fletcher loved having the opportunity to work with Niall and co. on their debut album (he wrote the ninth track, 'I Want'). 'They're a really likeable bunch of guys and they've got everything it takes to hit the big time,' he said. For One Direction's second album they worked together again, with Niall tweeting a photo of Tom playing a pink ukulele. He also tweeted: 'Great session today with @Dannymcfly @dougiemcfly @tommcfly, famous words of danny, "if we cant write a song, we'll have a laugh!" Haha.' They played computer games too – with the McFly boys coming out on top. Danny Jones, the band's guitarist, tweeted: 'Great sesh today with @Harry_Styles @NiallOfficial @Real_Liam_Payne @Louis_Tomlinson @zaynmalik1D Great hangin! shame about ya fifa skills!'

Niall and the other boys always enjoy filming their music videos, even though the whole process can last for many, many hours. While shooting their first ever video for 'What Makes You Beautiful' on a California beach they also recorded their own version of the Oasis classic 'Wonderwall', with Niall playing along on guitar. When fans heard it many of them started to cry. Superfan Emily Keeports tweeted: 'One Direction covered Wonderwall and i am crying tears of joy and perfectioness.' Megan Hurlbut felt just the same, tweeting: 'I'm listening to One Direction sing wonderwall right noow. Can't. handle. these. emotions. But seriously though, i'm like crying. #perfect.'

> ### DID YOU KNOW?
> When the boys were filming their first video they worked for 18 hours one day and 14 hours the next, so were left feeling shattered – and sunburnt! They still enjoyed chilling on the beach, though.

Louis got in a bit of trouble with a cop when they were filming 'What Makes You Beautiful' because he thought the cop had said to overtake him and he would follow from behind, but that wasn't what he said and it looked as if Louis was trying to make a quick getaway. Liam finds what happened really funny because Louis tried to joke around with the cop, but the cop was very serious and had his hand on his gun!

CHAPTER 8

SPECIAL MOMENTS

One of Niall's favourite events of 2011 was the night of the *GQ* Men of the Year awards, which were held at the Royal Opera House in London. There were so many huge stars there, from Charlize Theron to Dizzee Rascal, Emma Watson to Keith Richards. Niall told *GQ* magazine, 'Just being in the same room as Bono was great. Stephen Fry's speech was incredible as well.' Harry loved seeing actor Bill Nighy, and Liam was speechless when he spotted *Pirates of the Caribbean* star Johnny Depp.

DID YOU KNOW?

The boys all have alternative names that they call each other, which rhyme with their real ones. They call Harry 'Barry', Liam 'Ian', Niall 'Kyle', Louis 'Hughey' and Zayn is 'Wayne'. If Niall could change his name to anything else

> he joked to Louis that he would call himself 'Max Power' and Liam said he'd call himself 'Zayn Tomlinson'.

Afterwards, Harry went up to different celebrities including Pixie Lott and started to sing their songs to them and dance, full of confidence. Niall and the others didn't, however; they just chatted. They still find being famous so strange.

DID YOU KNOW?

Niall first met Emma Watson (who played Hermione in the *Harry Potter* movies) when One Direction were attending the *Deathly Hallows* première with the other *X Factor* singers on 11 November 2010. She came over to chat to them and wished them all the best, telling the cameras that she was rooting for them.

DID YOU KNOW?

The movies that make One Direction cry are *The Notebook*, *Click*, *Marley & Me* and *Finding Nemo*.

Niall is now a millionaire because One Direction have been so successful worldwide but you would never know it because he acts just like a normal teenager and he doesn't flash his cash around. He has never revealed in interviews how much money he has; if an interviewer asks he just says they get paid in jelly beans. In the past he has also joked that Simon Cowell is so successful because he is tight and keeps his money.

Another special moment for Niall and the other boys was when celebrating their second birthday on 23 July 2012. Niall wanted to thank their fans and tweeted: 'Guys its been 2 years today since we were formed, its been incredible

so far, its all down to you guys! Love you all soo much! Thank you.'

Zayn added: 'Wow 2 years, what an amazing journey and its all down to you guys. Thank you, sending my love to you all #2yearsof1d.'

All five of the lads were so grateful, they felt blessed to have made the final three in *The X Factor* 2010, to have released hit singles and an album, to have toured the world – it was better than they had ever imagined. Altogether their music videos had been viewed more than 350 million times!

A week after their second anniversary they were celebrating again, this time for selling 12 million records worldwide in one year. They sold eight million singles, three million albums and one million DVDs – an incredible amount. Their record label presented them with a special framed disc so they would have a lasting memento.

Liam told *Digital Spy*: 'We are obviously ecstatic and incredibly humbled. We have an incredible team of people around us who have helped us achieve this, and above all we would like to thank our fans. We owe all our success to them.'

DID YOU KNOW?

Niall and Liam decided to surprise fans who were shopping at the Westfield Shopping Centre, London by turning up unannounced and singing a duet version of 'What Makes You Beautiful'. Niall played guitar and they were supported by the shopping centre's house band, Soul Chango. The shoppers in the mall soon gathered around them and started taking photos and recording it on their mobile phones. After they'd finished the boys simply stood up and walked out towards the car park.

One of Niall's favourite moments of 2012 was winning a Brit Award for Best British Single for 'What Makes You Beautiful'. They were up against some great artists and songs: Adele and 'Someone Like You', Example and 'Changed The Way You Kissed Me', Jessie J and 'Price Tag', Ed Sheeran and 'The A Team', JLS and 'She Makes Me Wanna', Olly Murs and 'Heart Skips A Beat', The Wanted and 'Glad You Came' and the Military Wives for 'Wherever You Are'. Naturally the families of all the boys really wanted them to win. Harry's dad Des tweeted: 'Everything crossed for 1D at MTV's tonight, starts in a few hours. Best New Artist or Best Pop Video would be fab. Both would be a dream.'

DID YOU KNOW?

If they could choose anyone to be the sixth member of their band, One Direction would pick Ed Sheeran. Louis once had a dream that they had a sixth member and he wasn't very nice but the others wouldn't help him!

Their category at the Brits was so strong but because it was all down to the fans voting the boys thought they stood a chance. Niall had suspected, though, that Adele might win because she'd just picked up six Grammys. He revealed to CKO196.9 Radio: 'We had a great night! We had a great start to the night, great food, look around there's Rihanna over there, Bruno Mars is over here – it's crazy. And then they called our name out and we were just ecstatic, we couldn't believe it... like a Brit Award is the British version of a Grammy so it doesn't get much bigger than that in British music so we were honoured to collect that. And we did stay up all night – we went to the Sony after party and it was a good night. Noel Gallagher from Oasis, Chris Martin from Coldplay [were there].'

They also went to a McDonald's drive-through and Niall

ordered a quarter pounder with cheese, six chicken nuggets and a double cheeseburger! He was so happy with everything that had happened that night, and he loved getting to meet Danny O'Donoghue from The Script, an Irish band he really likes.

DID YOU KNOW?

Niall would love to collaborate with Bruno Mars, either on his own or with Harry, Liam, Louis and Zayn. He thinks he is an awesome musician and performer. He would also like to have the opportunity to sing with Jon Bon Jovi one day.

The bandmates had been presented with their award by English rapper Tinie Tempah and they had each been given the opportunity to say something if they wanted. Louis started them off, saying, 'Wow, we cannot believe that we are stood here on this stage! I wanna start off by saying this award is for the fans. We would be absolutely nowhere without them, so thank you so much.' He passed Harry the microphone and he said, 'We want to say a massive, again, thank you to the fans. Everything we do is for you and this is yours, so thank you so much and a massive thank you to Radio One.'

Liam was next, saying, 'You know obviously we'd be nobody without our team backstage, so we wanna thank all of them – Simon, Sony, everybody at Syco, Kim Davidson, Emma, everybody at Modest, thank you so much, Paul Higgins, all our team backstage. Thank you guys, you're amazing and to be on this stage is amazing and we're going to be doing our arena tour so we're massively flattered.'

Niall was the last to speak, summing up what the others had said: 'Again, thank you so much to everyone who voted for us. Our fans are absolutely incredible and again this is one for you.'

The boys were beaming from ear to ear as they left the stage, with Brits host James Corden telling them to ring their mums to let them know they'd be home late! Simon Cowell was thrilled for them and tweeted: 'Fantastic news. Congrats @onedirection I am very proud of you.'

DID YOU KNOW?

One Direction have been credited with saving the UK version of *The X Factor* from being axed. Simon Cowell explained to the *Daily Star* in May 2012: 'I thought, "If we don't find real stars, it's a waste of everyone's time". They're No 1 in 30 countries. That's when you realise it's really worth making this show.'

DID YOU KNOW?

If the boys had the opportunity to be Simon Cowell for a day, Niall would spent £20 million, just because he could. Harry would put on a 'I Love One Direction' hoodie and make sure the paparazzi saw him in it and Liam would put lots of money on a bouncy castle and jump on it!

Niall and the others didn't realise until later that Harry had accidentally thanked the wrong radio station in his speech. The award had been sponsored by Capital Radio, not Radio 1. It had been Capital listeners who had voted them the winners, so bosses at Capital were fuming. The boys' PR firm released a statement on Twitter the next day to apologise for the mistake. It read: 'One Direction forgot to thank the Capital Radio listeners last night when picking up their Brit Award for "Best British Single".

'This was an oversight as the boys were caught up in the excitement of winning.

'The band would like take this opportunity to thank Capital Radio and all their listeners for their support and for voting for them.'

Capital bosses still felt cheated, so they banned all One Direction tracks from being played on their station from that night (21 February 2012) and didn't book them for their Summertime Ball at Wembley Stadium. This ban last until approximately 7.45pm on 22 May 2012 when Capital Radio finally played the song!

Months later, when the boys were asked by *KansasCity.com* if they had met any other famous artists from Great Britain, Harry replied: 'We went to the Brit Awards. So there were loads of people there. We met like, Adele, Ed Sheeran. We met a lot of great British artists and we're very proud to be British.' Niall is proud to be Irish and will mention the fact that he is if any interviewers accidentally think they are all from England.

Another award ceremony that meant a lot to Niall and the rest of the boys was the 2012 Teen Choice Awards in the US. The band couldn't be there in person because they were recording in London but to win three awards meant the world to them and they left fans a pre-recorded message to thank them for voting. They also tweeted from their official account: 'Thanks Directioners for voting at #TCA12! We're so honored to take home 3 #ChoiceAwards including best love song: #WhatMakesYouBeautiful.' Our favourite boy band won the Choice summer music star group award, the Choice music breakout group and the Choice love song award. Their pre-recorded message was introduced by celebrity chef Gordon Ramsay; in it they all work together to make their surfboard award, as it had been posted to them in bits. It's very funny so if you haven't already seen it, you should check it out on YouTube.

Another one of Niall's favourite awards shows was the MTV

Video Music Awards in September 2012 – because they won three awards, and Katy Perry kissed him! None of the boys had expected to win; they all sent lots of tweets asking fans to vote for them and on the day itself Harry tweeted: 'Don't think I've ever been so nervous for anything. Can't wait for tonight!! VMAs!'

Niall told Australian radio hosts Kyle and Jackie O: 'Katy Perry had lovely purple lipstick on and I still haven't washed it off to be fair!' He tweeted a photo of their kiss and a message to Katy, saying: '@katyperry looks like its official me and you pic.Twitter.com/iYvge5Sb.' Altogether, it was tweeted over 77,000 times. Katy tweeted in response: 'I'll be your Mrs. Robinson.' (Mrs Robinson is a character from the 1967 movie *The Graduate*, starring Dustin Hoffman.)

When they'd won their first award the boys had gone backstage to their dressing room and Zayn told Niall, 'There's no way we can win a MTV Video Music Award and go home!' Niall agreed and so they stayed on in America for a few more days before flying home. Zayn managed to hurt his foot, though, so when they were getting the plane home the paparazzi took lots of photos. He wanted to reassure fans and so he tweeted: 'Hey guys, just to let you all know I'm all good, no need to worry aha', 'Just wanna take a moment to thank you guys for being so amazing' and 'I've said it so many times but ill say it again, you really are the best fans in the world, thank you for being so incredible. Love you all :x.'

In April 2012 Niall, Zayn, Liam, Louis and Harry were given the opportunity to appear as musical guests on the American hit comedy sketch show *Saturday Night Live* alongside host *Modern Family* star Sofia Vergara. It was a great honour as they would be following in the footsteps of Coldplay, Michael Bublé, Maroon 5, Kanye West and Rihanna, to name just a few. Over 37 million people watch the show every week, so it was a massive deal.

Niall told MTV before their performance: 'This is our kind of show. You know, we like to have a bit of a laugh. This is our perfect kind of show [and] we get involved as much as we can.' He also tweeted: 'vocal lesson and warm up with @HeleneHorlyck in a while. gettin ready for SNL tonight! gona be fun. also whos watchin iCarly tonight?'

Harry was excited, too, saying: 'I think a lot of it is gonna be a big adrenaline rush. The show's so big over here. I think it's going to be a lot of fun and I think we're gonna have as much fun with it as we can.'

On the night they performed 'What Makes You Beautiful' and 'One Thing'. They also acted in *The Manuel Ortiz Show* sketch, which required them to wear dodgy wigs, moustaches and to put on Spanish accents.

Afterwards Niall tweeted: 'SNL tonight was amazing. thanks to @nbcsnl for having us. much appreciated!'

Harry also sent a message, saying: 'Thank you so much to @nbcsnl for having us. That was a lot of fun and we'll never forget it.'

Going to Australia was unforgettable for Niall for many different reasons. Some of his family are over there so he could spend his days off with them, and he had loads of fun with the One Direction guys, too. His dad loved seeing the photos of Niall on a yacht in the newspapers back home. He is thrilled that Niall is having the time of his life with the other guys. Niall was gutted that they couldn't spend time with the fans at the airport when they arrived, tweeting: 'Australia we're here, sorry we couldn't come out, airport police said it wasn't safe, we really wanted to come out and say hi, cya soon [sic].' The same thing had happened when they arrived at LAX airport in January. Harry had tweeted that time, saying: 'Sorry that we couldn't stop at LAX guys.the US Marshall's said it wasn't safe. We all wanted to come see you .x.'

DID YOU KNOW?

As well as having family in Australia, Niall also has family in America. He has three cousins living over there – two called Katie and one called Annie. His youngest relative is Kaiden Jack Horan, who was born in Ireland in March 2012. Niall told his followers: 'Kaiden jack horan welcome to family buddie, first male horan born since me! Congrats daniel [Niall's first cousin] and mandy.'

After One Direction's first day in Australia, Niall tweeted: 'See you at sunrise tomorrow, OZ directioners! Off t sleep! Goodnight, great first day down under, gotta good feelin about this trip.'

Niall was right, the boys had an amazing trip. They performed a sell-out show in Sydney, went surfing, swimming and tried Vegemite for the first time. The only downside was some newspapers and websites printed stories saying that Harry and Liam were scared that they could have caught a disease after a koala they were holding urinated on them. The boys were understandably upset because there was no truth in the rumours at all; in fact, they had had a lovely day visiting the Lone Pine Koala Sanctuary.

One Direction were excited and a bit apprehensive when they discovered Ronan Keating wanted them to help him choose which groups to put through to the live shows on *The X Factor Australia* live shows. Ronan was keen to get the biggest band in the world to help him, and he knew that Niall and the boys would know exactly how the singers were feeling because they had been there themselves. They knew all about the tension and the pressure involved, and would be able to offer valuable advice as the groups' mentors. Ronan and the groups came to London for the 'home visits' round so the boys didn't have to fly out to

Australia. The Under 25 Girls, Under 25 Boys and Over 25s headed to New York, where Mel B had chosen Usher as the mentor for the Under 25 Boys, Australian actress Natalie Bassingthwaighte had chosen Ke$ha as the mentor for the Under 25 Girls and former Australian Idol winner Guy Sebastian had chosen Alicia Keys as the mentor for the Over 25s.

When Ronan introduced the groups to their mentors they were so excited they were cheering and clapping. One Direction must have felt relieved – Louis had been worried that when they appeared from behind the curtains they'd be met with silence. After a brief chat with all the groups, they had to get into position and get ready to hear each group's home visit performance. As they watched them perform they would look over at each other and then tell Ronan exactly what they thought. They particularly liked a girl group because they were gorgeous (one of them even winked at Harry), but in the end they helped Ronan choose The Collective (a boy band who sang Rihanna's 'We Found Love'), another boy band called Fourtunate (who sang Beyoncé's 'End of Time') and What About Tonight, a mixed group who sang 'Gives You Hell' by All-American Rejects. One Direction had inspired What About Tonight to audition for the *X Factor* so they were thrilled to get the chance to meet Niall, Harry, Zayn, Liam and Louis in person.

DID YOU KNOW?

When the band were interviewed for *X Factor Australia* they were asked if that day was their last day on earth how would they spend it? Niall said he would go for a pint with Ronan Keating, Harry decided to go up in a hot air balloon, Zayn said he would go see his family, then Niall said he wanted to swim with dolphins. Louis said they would do something high adrenaline, like skydive into their families' houses.

In May 2012, One Direction were excited to watch 'What Makes You Beautiful' being covered on the hit TV series *Glee*. It featured in the 'Prom-asaurus' episode and was sung by the actors who play Artie, Joe, Sam, Rory and Mike. When it was first announced in March that the *Glee* cast would be covering the song, Matthew Morrison (who plays teacher Will Schuester) told the *Sun*: 'I need to YouTube it to practise,' before joking, 'They've made it now though they're on *Glee*, this will probably help their record sales too.'

Niall and the boys decided they wanted their fans to be the first to see it, so tweeted on 4 May: '"What Makes You Beautiful" will make it's [sic] *Glee* US debut this Tuesday, 8 May. You can listen to the *Glee* version before it airs next week!'

Niall felt so honoured and told a journalist, 'To have a song in *Glee* is just fantastic! We're all big fans of the show and are so excited they chose "What Makes You Beautiful" for an episode.'

The *Glee* version of 'What Makes You Beautiful' charted at number 93 in Canada and number 162 in the UK. The cast also sang covers of Selena Gomez's 'Love You Like a Love Song', Ke$ha's 'Dinosaur', Berlin's 'Take My Breath Away' and Fergie's 'Big Girls Don't Cry' during the episode.

DID YOU KNOW?

One Direction are huge *X Factor USA* fans and love watching the shows on TV. Just before Series 2 launched Harry tweeted: 'Good luck to everyone on @thexfactorusa this year' and '1 day to wait! Hopefully we will get to meet you at some point.'

Louis tweeted: 'Loving @britneyspears's ruthless judging! #XFactorUSA' and Liam asked fans: 'Ready for @thexfactorusa tonight? I really want to see what @britneyspears is like as judge. Simon really likes her!'

CHAPTER 9

GIVING BACK

Niall is a very caring person and he likes to do what he can to help charities. Before he became famous he and his dad had their legs waxed in a local pub to raise money for charity. He found it very painful and wouldn't like to do it again!

When the *X Factor* finalists were asked whether they would like to do a charity single for Help for Heroes, they said 'yes' straight away. Niall knew that the money they raised when the single was released would go towards new recovery centres for injured soldiers and he went to meet recovering soldiers at the Headley Court Military Rehabilitation Centre to see firsthand how the money would be spent.

The song they would be releasing was a cover of the David Bowie track 'Heroes'. The original version had been released in 1977, but over the years lots of covers had

been done by artists such as Bon Jovi, Oasis and Nicole Kidman with Ewan McGregor.

When Niall and the other contestants were filming the video for their version, staff from Help for Heroes came to watch and gave the contestants the opportunity to ask any questions they might have. Niall told the *Sun*: 'It really puts things into perspective. We all complained about having to get up early and do this video shoot this morning – I feel so bad about that now. You don't realise how lucky you are. We're doing a huge TV show and other people have really, really tough jobs.'

Liam felt just the same, telling the reporter: 'I can't believe some of the people who fight out there are younger than me. It's so shocking that people our age can come back from places like Afghanistan disabled for ever. We're all really active in the band – we play football and work out all the time – the thought of not being able to do that is horrible.'

Niall enjoyed his first video shoot and looked forward to seeing it on TV. For the promotion of 'Heroes' all the contestants performed the track on the *X Factor* live show a few days later and it went straight to number one in the UK and Ireland. Zayn relayed how they were all feeling to Radio 1 host Reggie Yates when he said: 'It was pretty crazy when we were told we got to number one because it's for such a good cause and something we're all really proud about, that makes it so much better.'

In November 2011 they had the opportunity to sing on another *X Factor* charity single, this time raising money for the children's charity, Together For Short Lives. The boys, JLS and that year's *X Factor* finalists sang the Rose Royce track 'Wishing On A Star'. Simon Cowell released a statement which said: 'Having worked close hand with this charity and seeing the

amazing work they do for kids and their families who need help and support, I am thrilled that the *X Factor* charity single this year will benefit this charity.' The song was available for download on 27 November and for sale in shops the next day. It topped the UK charts on 4 December 2011, and raised thousands of pounds for the charity.

In May 2012 Niall and the boys were busy rehearsing for their American tour but they took time out to visit one of their biggest fans, schoolgirl Niamh Power. Niamh was suffering from cancer and sadly passed away on 6 July, but meeting Niall and Harry was perhaps one of the best days of her life. Harry and Niall went to see her in her hotel room and Niall later tweeted a photo and a message: 'Met this amazing girl this morning, Niamh! Great morning, brave girl.'

During their visit Harry gave her a kiss on the cheek and her mum told the *Daily Star*: 'She says she's never going to wash that cheek again. Niamh's smile was big enough to fill the room. Everyone in the band spent time talking to her. And the photo Niall put on Twitter has now gone round the world.'

Niall and the boys have visited many children who are sick through the children's charity Rays Of Sunshine, which helps to make the dreams of sick children come true. They met 11-year-old Tilly from Stoke on Trent, who is living with Spinal Muscular Atrophy, and 15-year-old Rebecca from Lancashire, who has cystic fibrosis. Rebecca was over the moon to meet the boys because she had been planning on attending one of their signings in the past with her friend but couldn't go because she had to go to hospital instead.

DID YOU KNOW?

The Rays Of Sunshine *Dish for a Wish Cook Book* contains the boys' recipe for nachos, as well as recipes

from JLS, Gordon Ramsay, Leona Lewis, Helena Bonham Carter and Gwyneth Paltrow, to name just a few. All money raised from the sales of the book go to the charity, so if you would like to buy one visit www.raysofsunshine.org.uk.

In July 2012 Niall helped British Airways raise £50,000 in partnership with Comic Relief by hosting a dinner date in the sky over London, along with Harry, Zayn, Liam and Louis. The boys pretended to be cabin crew and served their guests food and drink.

When he found out that One Direction would be headlining at the BBC Radio 1's Teen Awards in October 2012, Niall was thrilled because the awards recognise teenagers who have done incredible things as well as handing out music awards to artists. The awards were to be hosted by Harry's mate Nick Grimshaw and Taylor Swift, Little Mix, Conor Maynard and Ne-Yo would be performing. Niall told BBC *Newsbeat*: 'It was so much fun last year and it's a great line-up. It's always good to be on a great bill. And with the teen hero award, it's an award for people who have done amazing things. Obviously it's great to be part of that as well.'

The boys picked up three awards on the night: Best British Single for 'One Thing', Best British Album for *Up All Night* and Best British Music Act.

CHAPTER 10

TOURING

Niall loves playing pranks on the other lads while they are asleep. When they are on tour they have to sleep in their van a lot as they drive from venue to venue and so Niall and the others like to have fun. Harry once shaved his initials into Zayn's leg hair and Zayn shaved a slit in Liam's eyebrow. They never do anything too radical because they don't want to get into trouble with their management. Louis once pranked Niall when he was buying a burger – he just went over and pulled his trousers down!

DID YOU KNOW?

Harry and Niall think they are the best dancers in the band; Louis thinks he's the most stylish.

The biggest prank the band has ever done was so amazing that

Niall will never, ever forget it. Louis and Zayn managed to trick Harry into thinking that he was helping a woman giving birth during an interview. The boys were on Nickelodeon and there was an actress playing the part of the heavily pregnant producer. They were sitting on couches with her as she explained that when her baby is kicking her bladder she likes to sing to calm her down, and she asked whether they would sing for her. They started to sing 'Rock-a-bye baby'. She then started to cry out 'in pain' and Louis was sent to ring his mum because she is a nurse. When she shouted out, 'This baby is coming out right now!', Harry looked so shocked but together with Zayn, he went over to help her stand. Niall and Liam were completely lost, looking at each other as if to say, 'What do we do?' Louis ran back in and suggested that she should lie on the floor. Harry looked over, asking, 'Why is no one, why is no one here?'

Niall was sent to try and get help – still thinking the woman was really having a baby. Liam and Harry kept shouting for him to get people to help, while the woman was asking for them to ring her husband. Harry was so good with her, even mimicking how she should breathe. Liam rang her husband but got cut off so he ended up leaving a voicemail message. Harry couldn't help but laugh when she said that she'd farted. He was flabbergasted when the woman announced, 'You've all been pranked by Nickelodeon!'

Louis and Zayn were so happy that the others fell for it that they high-fived each other and Harry covered his head in shock. Later he told the camera: 'I was actually thinking this is going to be a great press story – One Direction deliver a child!'

DID YOU KNOW?

Whenever he can, Niall likes to have lie-ins and catch up on his sleep. One day he tweeted: 'ragin! missed the

ireland game coz i was too busy being a lazy fool and sleeping!' He'd missed Ireland playing Italy in Euro 2012. Ireland won 2-0.

The boys' tour manager is Irishman Paul Higgins and they are all very close to him. Paul used to work with Boyzone, Westlife, Girls Aloud and former *X Factor* winner Shayne Ward. He coordinates all the bodyguards and makes sure the bandmates have adequate cover when they visit different countries. The boys have thanked him in awards speeches and went over to Ireland for Paul's wedding. While there they filmed a 'marryoke' with Paul, his new wife Clodagh and the rest of their guests. Niall and Liam mimed the song 'My Perfect Day' and Harry, Louis and Zayn joined them for 'I've Gotta Feeling'. To see the videos, just search 'Marryoke – Paul and Clodagh' on YouTube. If you want to follow Paul on Twitter, his Twitter account is @paulyhiggins. According to Niall, Paul is the fourth most followed Irishman on Twitter!

Niall and the rest of One Direction love having full-on scraps with Paul, but one day a fight went horribly wrong when Paul's watch caught Niall's hand and split his thumb! The gash went right down the thumb and was horribly bloody. Niall wasn't too concerned and minutes later he was back fighting. The wound has left a scar that you can make out if you look closely at his thumb.

DID YOU KNOW?

At comedian/actor James Corden's wedding in September 2012 Niall and Louis accidentally turned up wearing the same suit. They each had a charcoal grey Kooples suit on, with a white shirt, so they looked like twins. The boys couldn't believe it – they each have lots

of suits so it was strange that they picked the same one. However, they didn't let it spoil the day and let the other guests make fun of them. Olympic bronze medallist Tom Daley tweeted a photo of the three of them with the message: 'Yes they are wearing the same suits!!! Haha @niallofficial @louis_tomlinson.'

Niall is really scared of pigeons and the *Sun* reported that extra security had been put in place during their tour of America to make sure that no pigeons came close to him. He told the newspaper: 'I get really nervous if pigeons are flying around before shows. I can't stand them after one once flew in through my bathroom window and went for me while I was having a wee. That was enough. I think pigeons target me.'

Harry added: 'Niall's really scared of pigeons – we have to protect him.'

DID YOU KNOW?

In one of their video diaries the boys had a pretend pigeon that they nicknamed Kevin and it sat on Niall's knee.

On 4 January 2012 the boys were involved in a road accident on the way back to their hotel after performing at The National Indoor Arena, Birmingham. The *Sun* reported that a car had hit them at 30mph and a source claimed: 'It was a close call; the lads and their two tour managers were pretty shaken up and were treated for varying degrees of whiplash. Yesterday they were seen by an osteopath who gave them the all-clear.'

The boys didn't miss any gigs, travelling down to Plymouth

as planned the very next night. Niall understood that fans might be worried so he tweeted to reassure them: 'Guys, thanks for all your messages. We were involved in a really minor accident. We are all absolutely fine!'

He was looking forward to the Plymouth performance, later tweeting 'Green army! Wana hear ya loud tonight! Its gona be fun! #1DinPlymouth.'

Niall and the boys love having the opportunity to tour the world and they really enjoy performing in front of One Direction's international fans. While in America they performed at New York's Radio City Hall, which was a truly memorable performance. Louis enthused to MTV: 'It was absolutely incredible to play Radio City Hall; that place has got a lot of history and it was just such an honour to play in front of that crowd.'

Before they perform a gig, the One Direction boys feel what Niall describes as 'a relaxed kind of nervous'. It's during the walk from their dressing room to the stage that the nerves hit them, rather than when they are onstage. Louis explained to *KansasCity.com*: 'We kind of get nervous, like even if we have a big show to do we don't get nervous until about five minutes before we all kind of give each other words of good luck and try and make each other kind of laugh.'

When Niall and the boys did their first gigs they used to get more freaked out before they went onstage, but now they perform to thousands of people they feel much better because the noise of the crowd helps calm their nerves. Niall loves it when he's performing and the watching fans are really loud, screaming and singing along. He and the rest of the boys find it strange when they say 'Hello, New York', 'Hello, Dublin' or 'Hello, London' because they don't feel mega famous, they feel so blessed. When they were leaving Radio City Hall that particular night, fans surrounded their van, jumping on its

back bumper and banging on the windows. Security had to force the girls back so they could drive away. Before they did, the boys just had to wait so Niall decided to have a pretend fight with Liam!

DID YOU KNOW?

People throw strange things at the boys when they are performing on stage. When they were playing in Houston, USA, a fan threw an iPhone at Niall with her house key and a rude note sellotaped to it. He only saw it at the last second because he was blinded by the lights and he had to knock it away from him, otherwise he thought it would smash his collarbone. Yikes! Another fan threw a walkie-talkie on the stage and was talking through the other one, so when Harry picked it up, he was like 'Hello?' and she was talking back. Niall thought that was really clever.

The boys headed to a bowling alley to celebrate but ended up enjoying themselves too much. They started messing around, throwing three balls at once, and broke the lane machinery. Louis confessed to the *Mirror*: 'The whole thing came off its hinges. It totally broke. We got a slap on the hand and were told off by the label for that.'

Harry added: 'It was really bad but quite funny – but no one else thought so.'

The boys have nearly got into trouble at other times too, but have managed to get away with it. They tried to trash a Winnebago during their tour of America but they couldn't pull it off. Harry told the *Sun*: 'Everyone was saying we weren't very rock 'n' roll. I thought I'd throw a TV out of the Winnebago window.'

Louis added: 'It didn't smash – it didn't even have one scratch on it.'

At a video shoot they did, Zayn was driving a red moped but he crashed it, causing quite a bit of damage. He confided in *Celebs On Sunday* magazine: 'I smashed up a Vespa. I'm making this sound more glamorous than it actually was. It just span out and went crazy, ran on about two metres and hit some gravel. And it was a limited edition, worth thousands. They had to put red nail polish on it to cover the scratches.'

Liam added: 'He'd never driven a moped before and he had this brand new red one we were using in a video shoot – and crashed it.'

During their UK and Ireland tour the band was supported by American soft-rock band Boyce Avenue, made up of brothers Alejandro, Daniel and Fabian Manzano. When the *Up All Night* tour finished, Boyce Avenue wanted to give the boys something to remember them by so they presented them with customised baby Taylor guitars with 1D & BA on the back and their autographs. Each one had the name of the person it belonged to and a short message. Niall was so happy when they presented him with his that he gave them a big hug. The guitars will have cost Boyce Avenue a massive £20,000! To follow the boys on Twitter go to @BoyceAvenue.

Lead singer Daniel Manzano told the *Daily Star* in July 2012: 'We're meeting up to see what they think of some ideas we've got for them. We've got a studio right by the beach, so it's a cool place for bands to come and write with us.' Sadly, no tracks from their second album *Take Me Home* were written by Boyce Avenue but they might possibly work with One Direction in the future.

DID YOU KNOW?

In 2010 Boyce Avenue was the second most searched band on YouTube with over 600 million views.

Sometimes Niall's days off can be a bit crazy and during one such day in New York he ended up being hit in the face by a fan. Niall and Liam had decided to explore the city together but they were mobbed. Liam's shirt was ripped and both had their hair pulled according to a source from the *Mirror*, who said: 'They couldn't see where they were going and it was really, really dangerous. Nearby police had to calm the girls down.

'They are going to have to be more careful in the future and have at least a security guard each with them. It's a shame for the boys because they appreciate their freedom.'

Niall and Liam were both shocked by what happened. Niall tweeted: 'This is a complete joke... ridic... Day off, wana chill', while Liam commented: 'That wasn't even funny.' The boys knew that it was just a minority of fans who had ruined their day off and later Niall sent a tweet to let the fans outside their hotel know that he could hear them singing.

DID YOU KNOW?

When Niall gets days off in London he likes to do nothing. 'I just sit on the couch – like I've done for the past three or four days in London,' he confessed to the *Mirror*. 'I only left the house once to go and buy a bottle of water. I just sat there, playing my guitar, putting my feet on the table and watching television.'

Harry, Zayn, Liam and Louis are the opposite: they prefer to do things on their days off. But for Niall days off are about relaxing

and taking it easy. When he had to wear braces on his teeth, he would quite often have to go to the dentist on his days off because it was hard to fit in appointments. He once told Louis that if he hadn't been in One Direction he might have become a dentist. Niall was so excited after visiting the dentist on 14 August 2012 that he tweeted fans to let them know what the dentist had told him: 'Been to dentist today! got them tightened up and stuff! he tells me i will be gettin braces off in 6 months...teeth moving fast! sick.'

Whenever he has some spare time when he's abroad, Niall likes to catch up on the football matches back home and uses a Sky Sports App on his phone to watch them. The Sky App is definitely his favourite app. He once had a dream that he was playing in the Champions League Final – with Didier Drogba!

If the weather is good Niall likes to go out and make the most of it. He has told his fans via Twitter: 'Wohoooo suns out again! Loving it! Shorts are on, bringing the chicken legs out!' and 'Goodmorning! Ive looked out the window and decided im gona have a bbq today.' He likes to play golf with the other members of One Direction or his friends. After playing against JLS band member Marvin he tweeted: 'Just played golf with marv! Great laugh! I split my trousers right down the middle on the first hole, tie'n my laces hahaha! #fool.'

One of the band's best days off in America was when they visited the Six Flags Magic Mountain theme park in Los Angeles. They got to enjoy some massive rides and Niall tweeted: 'Went to six flags today with the lads, had a great laugh! some scary rollercoasters there! But it was fun!'

DID YOU KNOW?

When Harry was younger he used to be scared of going on rollercoasters.

They also went fishing together in California and Liam caught a baby tiger shark. He's not an experienced angler, so he did really well. After they'd all admired his catch he released it. The boys were accompanied by their backing musicians: Josh Devine, Sandy Beales, Jon Shone and Dan Richards. California is one of Niall's favourite places to visit because the weather is good and the pace of life relaxed rather than rushed. He also likes Italy because he loves Italian food.

Sandy tweeted: 'Ridiculous night out on a boat in San Diego, @Real_Liam_Payne even caught a shark, yeah a shark, It's my main phobia but I gave it a stroke.'

Josh also tweeted, saying: 'Had a late night fishing trip @Real_Liam_Payne caught a baby tiger shark. felt very weird to touch such a killer.'

Josh, Sandy, Jon and Dan enjoy a really close friendship with the boys and they have their own fans too. They have met Will Smith, Katy Perry, Seal, Bear Grylls and many more top stars. When they were in Milwaukee, Sandy went to see his friends and ended up doing a skydive without telling Niall. Niall would love to skydive and was gutted that he missed out but he doesn't think he'd be allowed to do it when the boys are touring just in case he injures himself.

BAND FACT FILE

Josh Devine: drummer

Josh is from Bournemouth and started playing the drums when he was three. He passed his Grade 8 drum qualification when he was still in school and competed in numerous drumming competitions, winning Toni Cannelli's national drum competition Beat in 2007 when he was only 15. A year later he was a finalist in the

Mapex Drummer of Tomorrow competition and won the technical category. He has been a studio drummer for many years now, working with For all my Valentines, Charlee Drew, Fandangle and rapper Skepta. When he became One Direction's drummer Josh was really excited and his first performance was on the ITV show *Red or Black?* – One Direction's first performance of their first single, 'What Makes You Beautiful'. Josh went outside to chat to fans that were waiting patiently to see if Niall and the boys would come out but they thought he was just an audience member! His Twitter account is: @JoshDevineDrums

Sandy Beale: bass guitarist
On his official website Sandy states that he specialises in electric, upright and synth bass. He lives in London when he's not touring with One Direction and was chosen for *Bass Guitar Magazine*'s 'bass to the future' feature. Sandy trained at the Tech Music School in London. He is also the musical director for singer/songwriter Leddra Chapman. Going on the road with One Direction was his first major tour. Sandy and the rest of the band like having a mess around and filmed a funny clip of themselves playing pipes while dressed as leprechauns. To view Sandy's backstage videos, check out his YouTube channel. His Twitter account is: @sandybeales

Jon Shone: musical director/keys
Jon is a keyboard tutor at the Tech Music School and has worked with many top artists. He was the musical director for Marina & the Diamonds when they were supporting Katy Perry on her *California Dreams* World Tour. As the

musical director for One Direction he was in charge of putting together the band and he found Sandy, Josh and Dan after auditioning around 60 top musicians. He loved their energy and that they were young guys. To prepare, they had two weeks of intense rehearsals before the production rehearsals with Niall, Zayn, Liam, Louis and Harry. Jon's keyboards are lots of fun to play, so in rehearsals he has to watch that Niall doesn't sneak a go when his back is turned! His Twitter account is: @JonShoneKeys

Dan Richards: guitarist

As well as playing the guitar himself, Dan is a guitar teacher and composes his own music. He has a Masters in popular music performance from the London College of Music and has worked with lots of artists over the past 10 years. Dan plays guitar in the acoustic version of 'One Thing'. Both Dan and Sandy have a BMus (Hons) degree from the Tech Music School. Before they went on tour with the band, Jon was interviewed for the school website and he said: 'It's great having Sandy and Dan on board. They are both young, with professional attitudes, and that goes a long way in the session world. Reliability is key when preparing for a tour and I'm really looking forward to starting rehearsals with the guys.' Dan's Twitter account is: @guitarmandan

DID YOU KNOW?

While One Direction were in the States they missed food from home. Niall craved Irish sausages and English breakfast tea (with three sugars).

In July 2012 the boys were doing a photoshoot

and Harry nearly choked. He tweeted: 'Good shoot today!! Long day but some great shots, hope you guys like them x

'But I did throw a blueberry to the back of my mouth an choked.'

One fan was quick to reply, telling him: 'I'll give you mouth to mouth if you need it!!! :)'

DID YOU KNOW?

The boys tried to convince their management to let them have a dog on tour but this wasn't allowed.

Niall loved having Ollys Murs as their supporting act while they were touring America because he is such a good mate. Olly came second in the *X Factor* in Series 6, the year before One Direction auditioned, and had co-hosted the *Xtra Factor* show with Caroline Flack from Series 8. He was glad that he had the opportunity to travel with the band for six weeks and that One Direction fans liked him. At the time he told *USA Today* jokingly: 'The [One Direction] fans are insane! Running after the bus, jumping from trashcans, just so infatuated with the guys. One Direction fans wanted to know who I was. American fans are brilliant!'

Olly was shocked when he found out that some fans of Niall and the boys will search through the garbage bins to get hold of their rubbish. It was much more extreme than anything he'd seen before.

DID YOU KNOW?

One day while they were chilling out Olly and Niall decided to do an acoustic version of Olly's track 'Heart Skips A Beat'. You should check it out on YouTube – just

search 'Olly Murs Niall Horan Heart Skips a Beat'. Olly
and a few other people are in the dressing room singing,
but Niall doesn't appear straight away – only when the
cameraman spins round to reveal Niall sitting on the toilet
with his guitar, playing and singing away!

In another interview, this time with MTV, Olly said: 'One
Direction's fans, they literally found out I was supporting them,
they went online, found out who I was, what songs I've done,
my videos and then I walked out [at the] first gig in Detroit
[and] everyone's just crazy. I was like, "This is insane. They don't
even know who I am. How could they be doing this?"'

Niall might have been a long way from home when they
were touring America and Canada but his mum came along for
two weeks. He loved treating her and insisted she didn't pay for
a thing. Although he likes it when his parents visit him
sometimes he finds it difficult not being able to do what he
wants because he's catering for them. When one of his friends
comes over of course it's different because they just tag along
with whatever Niall and the One Direction boys are doing.

Maura told the *Mirror*: 'I brought Niall to America 14 years
ago and he brought me this time around – I didn't put my hand
in my pocket at all, I've never had that in my life.' She loved
hearing girls shouting her son's name and it made her feel very
proud. Maura can't believe how much life has changed for
Niall since One Direction was formed: 'It's mind-blowing. Last
weekend he met the Obamas, so the child's mind must be
blown with what he's getting to see and do.'

And she was right. Niall was star-struck when he met Michelle
Obama for the first time. He thought she looked incredible and
he's a big fan of Barack Obama so it was a surreal experience.

Above: One Direction leaving the *X Factor* studios after a hectic day.

Below: A far cry from their *X Factor* days; accepting an award at the MTV Video Music Awards in Los Angeles.

Niall tried Vegemite on toast for the first time on the breakfast show *Sunrise* in Australia. He tried one bite and didn't like it. The rest of the toast was auctioned on eBay for a staggering $65,000.

Above: Talking to fans.

Below: Taking time out from the One Direction rollercoaster relaxing on a boat.

Niall loves to play the guitar. In concert at Radio City, New York.

Above: Niall and the band celebrating St. Patrick's day.

Below: Arriving at Heathrow Airport after a busy tour of the US.

Above and below: At the MTV Video Music Awards in Los Angeles. Niall wanted to thank Katy Perry for supporting him during the *X Factor* auditions.

DID YOU KNOW?

Harry, Liam, Louis and Zayn decided to commission a waxwork of Barack Obama for Niall's 18th birthday present. Liam explained why to the *Sun*: 'Niall is obsessed with Barack Obama. He knows everything about him. We looked around for the waxwork for ages. It's a life-size model and it's heavy.

'We had it made and delivered. We all chipped in for it. He sits on a bench in our flat. Niall loves it.'

The boys kept how much it cost a secret from Niall. He thought it was a great gift and hoped they might get him a matching 'Michelle' waxwork for his 19th birthday. He decided to keep it on his balcony to confuse people when they looked up, but that was a big mistake as the wind and rain damaged it.

Liam, Louis, Zayn and Niall told Capital Radio that they would like to buy Harry a Mick Jagger waxwork for one of his birthdays. The press have suggested that Harry looks like Mick did when he was younger, saying he could be his dad. Des, Harry's real father, can't have been too happy to hear that!

The celebrity that Niall most likes to chat to is Katy Perry because she makes him laugh every time they meet at awards shows. Katy likes him (and the rest of One Direction) too, as she admitted to the *Irish Sun*: 'They've been so sweet to me every time I meet them, they're like the biggest thing in the world right now. I'm thrilled for the success they're enjoying and love hanging out with them – Niall is just lovely.'

DID YOU KNOW?

When One Direction were touring, Niall did a cover of 'Stereo Hearts' by Gym Class Heroes. They found out and tweeted, 'Shout out to our boy @niallofficial in @onedirection for covering stereo hearts during your set!'

Niall responded: '@GymClassHeroes yo! Thanks guys! Its a great song, love doin it. Hope I'm doin it justice! Haha! Much love, hope to see you soon.'

On the last night of their *Up All Night* tour in Fort Lauderdale, Florida, all the boys were feeling emotional. Harry tweeted: 'Last show of the tour tonight. Thanks to an amazing crew, and everyone involved for making it what it was. Tonight will be fun.' They had performed over 60 shows worldwide, something they had never expected when the UK and Ireland dates had been announced.

Niall summed up how they were all feeling in his tweet after the concert: 'Wow ft,lauderdale! Great way to finish our 1st headline US tour! #upallnight tour is done! Long 6 months but amazing! Thank you all so much.'

Olly Murs took the opportunity to thank the boys publicly for letting him be their support act, tweeting: 'What a buzz its been @onedirection can't thank you guys enough! Was superb! Loved America!! Been wicked. See you lads in the UK!!!'

After they got back to the UK, Niall decided to go on holiday with his friends and family to Marbella, Spain. They stayed at The Ocean Club and had a great time chilling out in the pool and the jacuzzi. The paparazzi took lots of photos of Niall, which was a shame because he just wanted to relax and be himself, not a famous pop star.

When the *Up All Night* Tour DVD was due to be released in May 2012, the boys decided to perform a surprise gig in an American diner for fans. Niall explained to the backstage *VEVO Go* session camera: 'With today's *Go Show* the fans, again, don't know we're coming. They think they're here to watch the DVD of our tour so we're gonna go in and surprise them.'

The girls were sitting in booths or on stools by the counter and were speechless when Louis, Liam, Zayn, Niall and Harry appeared from a back door. With just an acoustic guitar supporting them, they sang 'What Makes You Beautiful'. Some of the girls couldn't help but smile at each other and sing along. Liam and Louis picked up ketchup bottles and pretended they were microphones. Niall got the girls to clap along and after Harry finished singing the last line, they gave the girls on the stools high-fives before leaving.

Outside Harry told the cameras: 'I think when we play to like, intimate crowds, I think a lot of our songs are really fun and, kind of, high energy, so when we do it acoustic it's nice to kinda slow it down and have less people and just, you know, make it a little more personal and less about the atmosphere and more about the people in the room.'

Niall added: 'It's the people you get there, you get a natural reaction out of them because it's much more relaxed and, you know, they feel a bit more privileged or whatever to be in a smaller room with just us. So it's quite nice.'

DID YOU KNOW?

The song that Niall most relates to on the album is the title track 'Up All Night' because it sums up who One Direction are and what they like doing. They like staying up really late together; they enjoy partying when they're

in London and chilling out too. He also likes 'One Thing' because everyone knows someone who has that special something that you can't put your finger on.

As well as fans being able to buy the tour DVD, they could also watch it on TV as it was broadcast on Nickelodeon on 25 August at 5.30pm. In a statement Harry told fans: 'The *Up All Night* tour was our first headline tour and it was such a special moment in our career. We're very excited to be able to share this moment with Nickelodeon viewers.'

CHAPTER 11

RIVALS

After the boys went over to America, a US band (also called 'One Direction') came out and said they wanted the boys to stop using their name. In April 2012 they launched a legal challenge, suing for $1 million in damages. They claimed in having the same name the band was confusing fans. The US One Direction soon began receiving angry tweets from fans of Niall, Liam, Louis, Harry and Zayn.

Niall and the boys really didn't want to change their name because they had been One Direction since the very beginning. They didn't want to have to start again with a new name, or with one they didn't like as much, but they had to wait and see what happened. Their families believed they should keep the name too. Niall's dad Bobby told a reporter that they had worked hard to crack America with the name so they should keep it.

In June 2012 the news broke that Simon Cowell was countersuing the US One Direction. According to the *Hollywood Reporter* Syco and Sony were arguing that the US One Direction had 'devised and perpetrated a scheme to exploit the goodwill' of our favourite boy band, and it was actually Niall's band who were more likely to miss out on revenue because of the confusion. The US One Direction had tried to say they were out first because their album, *The Light*, had been released on iTunes in February 2011 – more than a year before Niall's band released their first album in the US. However, Syco and Sony argued that YouTube videos of the group in the UK *X Factor* had been viewed worldwide since September 2010.

The two bands reached an agreement on Tuesday, 4 September 2012, with the US band changing their name. They wrote on their Facebook page: 'The California band formerly known as One Direction, whose albums are titled *The Light* and *Uncharted Shores*, will now be known as Uncharted Shores.'

DID YOU KNOW?

While the boys were touring America and Australia, they had to phone home a lot as they were away from their families and friends for weeks on end. In May 2012 the *Mirror* reported that their phone bills had been £14,000 ($22,144) and their record label were not amused. The bills were so high because the boys use their phones to update their Twitter and Facebook accounts. The *Mirror*'s source also said that Niall and Liam called home a lot because they got homesick. In the end their bills were paid off for them but they were told to be more careful in the future.

Niall is great friends with Liam, Louis, Zayn and Harry, and always will be, no matter what. All five members of One Direction are determined to stay together and became very close during their first tour. When they first started out, the British press claimed that Niall, Zayn and Louis were jealous of Liam and Harry because they were getting more airtime on *The X Factor.* This wasn't the case at all. Different members of One Direction are the most popular depending on which country they are in, with Niall being the most popular in America and Canada. In fact all five lads have thousands upon thousands of fans, so they don't mind at all.

Niall's older brother Greg talked to his local paper, the *Herald*, about the jealousy rumours while Niall was on *The X Factor.* 'It's absolute nonsense,' he said. 'The boys all get on really well together. They instantly bonded and have become the best of friends. I'm so proud of Niall – he is getting on great. He rang a few times during the week but I don't want to talk to him because I just miss him so much. He is loving every second of the experience and the lads are all fantastic; they have a huge amount of respect for each other. They have gelled so well that it's like they have already known each other for 10 years.'

One of the daftest rumours Niall has heard was that he'd got married. He tweeted on 25 September 2012: 'Hahhaha I was gettin mentions and dm's last night askin me if I was married! Hahahahah heard it all now! People actually believe this stuff.' The worst rumours that the boys have heard are that they died on the way to their second video shoot and that Harry had been arrested!

CHAPTER 12

TAKE ME HOME

Recording the second album was extra pressure because the first one had been so good, but Niall and the boys couldn't wait to start writing and recording new material. After one good session Niall tweeted: 'What a sick day in the studio! Got loads of vocal down and recorded 2 songs! On guitar! #worldtour2013 #cantwait.'

He tweeted on 30 June: 'Lets have more fun! Im lying on my bunk on the bus outside a recording studio, thinking, we're recording album 2 already! #1Dalbum2.'

Niall and the boys wanted their second album to have more guitars in it than the first album, *Up All Night*, and they were keen to work with Ed Sheeran again. Liam told the *Daily Star*: 'Ed is such a talented guy. We spoke to him about helping again for the next album, which we want to actually write with him this time.

He gave us almost a whole album of songs to choose from last time; there were so many of his songs that we wanted to record.'

Louis added: 'We like the sound of a real guitar on tour, we beefed up the live show so now we want to take it onto the album.'

They also wanted to write more tracks themselves, as Harry revealed to the *Sun*: 'We're always writing on the road and in hotels and airports. We don't ever want our music to sound like a 40-year-old man in an office has written it and given it to us to perform.'

Niall had a lot of input on the album, as he explained to MTV in the summer leading up to its release: 'The way it works for us, I don't know how everyone else works, but people don't see the meetings that we do, the all-day meetings about the album, and the way the songs are going to be even listed on the back of the album and album artwork.

'We want to have the most control that we possibly can of everything that we do. Like at the moment, I'm just proofreading the single artwork for the next single. They don't see that.'

At first fans thought that the single One Direction were to release first was called 'Heartbreaker', but Niall set the record straight by saying that there wasn't even a song called 'Heartbreaker' on the album. Someone had just made it up and it had been spread on Twitter. It turned out that the first track they were to release from their second album, *Take Me Home*, was 'Live While We're Young'. Fans could pre-order it from Friday, 24 August 2012 and it was to be released on 30 September, although it ended up being released earlier. It was written by Savan Kotecha, Rami Yacoub and Carl Falk, the three guys behind 'What Makes You Beautiful'.

Fans didn't know what it would sound like, but they knew

that Niall and co. wouldn't let them down. Niall told fans on Twitter: 'Love the fact "live while we're young" is still trending! Since 1pm uk time! That is unbelievable! U guys are incredible! Love you so much.'

The next day he added: 'Guys! Loving the love for LWWY! Amazing pre orders! Keep buying! Keep eyes and ears open, we're coming back!'

Instantly it became the fastest-selling pre-order single ever, number one in a phenomenal 40 countries worldwide from the UK to New Zealand, Singapore to Mexico. The boys' PR company released a statement on their website, stating: '"Live While We're Young" sees the global superstars once again teaming up with songwriters Savan Kotecha, Rami Yacoub & Carl Falk and the result is unmistakeably One Direction. "Live While We're Young" is pop perfection – an immediate, energy packed song mixing rock undertones with smooth harmonies, about living for the moment.'

Niall tweeted: 'Thanks for the love for LWWY, we have worked hard on this album, hope u enjoy the rest of it.'

The boys filmed the video for 'Live While We're Young' in the Kent countryside over two days. Harry tweeted: 'Great day shooting for the music video for "Live While We're Young" bit nippy.'

The video was directed by Vaughan Arnell, who had previously directed the Spice Girls' 'Say You'll Be There' video and several Robbie Williams' videos, including 'Somethin' Stupid' with Nicole Kidman and 'Rock DJ'. It was a feelgood video, with the boys waking up in a huge tent at the beginning and then having fun with their friends around a camp. They have waterfights, play in a pool, Louis drives them around in a jeep going really fast; they play football, swing off a rope swing, go on a raft, play in inflatable balls and generally have lots of

fun. Niall plays his guitar and even appears without a top on – whereas the other boys just keep their soaking shirts on.

After they'd finished filming Niall tweeted: 'Guys! We have literally just finished shooting the video for "live while we're young" ur gona love it! It was soo fun to shoot!'

Harry added: 'Day two finished, and that's the video for "Live While We're Young" done. Amazing crew, amazing people involved. Thanks again.'

The boys wanted to keep the video under wraps until the official unveiling on 24 September 2012, but this wasn't to be – photos from the video were leaked online in August and on 20 September someone posted a rough version of the whole video online. Rather than have fans be disappointed, they decided to publish the official, finished version that day. In a statement released they said: 'We wanted our fans to see the video and hear the single in the proper way so we've moved the premiere to tonight. We're really excited about LWWY, we've worked really hard on it and we can't wait for everyone to see and hear it later today!'

DID YOU KNOW?

The video for 'Live While We're Young' beat the record for the most number of views in 24 hours after it was watched 8.24 million times. The VEVO (an online video website) title had previously been held by Justin Bieber's video for 'Boyfriend', which had been watched 8 million times after it was released on 3 May 2012.

One Direction's PR company added: 'The eagerly awaited second album is due for release in November 2012 and sees One Direction collaborating with a whole host of first-class writers and producers. As well as reuniting with the likes of

Rami Yacoub & Carl Falk and Savan Kotecha, Ed Sheeran and McFly's Tom Fletcher, the album features input from Dr Luke, Shellback and Toby Gad. The album is sure to be another huge smash release from a truly international pop phenomenon.'

DID YOU KNOW?

Niall had to pull out of one of the recording sessions for *Take Me Home* because he lost his voice. He tweeted: 'Waking up with no voice! Nooo... Sick day today! Now off to sleep.' After resting for a while he tweeted: 'Guys love you all soo much! We been in the studio lately! We're comin back with more music in the next couple of months! Get ready.'

Take Me Home track list:
1. 'Live While We're Young'
2. 'Kiss You'
3. 'Little Things'
4. 'C'mon, C'mon'
5. 'Last First Kiss'
6. 'Heart Attack'
7. 'Rock Me'
8. 'Change My Mind'
9. 'I Would'
10. 'Over Again'
11. 'Back for You'
12. 'They Don't Know About Us'
13. 'Summer Love'

The album cover they chose for *Take Me Home* had Niall inside a traditional red phone box making a call, with Harry standing with his arms crossed outside, looking up at Liam, who is lying

on the top of the phone box with his legs dangling down, looking as if he's about to fall off. Louis sits on Zayn's shoulder, reaching up to grab onto Liam's arm.

Niall was looking forward to performing from the album at a special headline gig at Madison Square Garden in New York on 3 December 2012. He told the press: 'We are so happy to be playing Madison Square Garden. To be headlining our OWN show in a venue that has played host to countless legendary acts that we have grown up listening to and adore is obviously a dream come true for us all. We can't wait to play for our fans on 3 December.'

Before the album was released it was top secret, but the British girl group Little Mix got to hear a sneak preview because Perrie Edwards from the band was dating Zayn. Jade Thirlwall from the group confessed to Capital FM: 'I heard one. We heard a cheeky little song, but we're not allowed to say anything. It's brilliant! The fans will love it.'

Leigh-Anne Pinnock, who would like to work with Niall, Harry, Zayn, Liam and Louis, added: 'I think it would be really interesting — a Little Mix and One Direction [song]. Imagine what that would be like.'

Jesy Nelson wasn't sure, however, telling the radio host: 'I think we have different styles of music so I don't know how we would make it work. It might work — you never know.'

DID YOU KNOW?

When Little Mix were on *The X Factor* One Direction wanted them to win. They thought they were different to other girl groups who had appeared on the show in the past — and Zayn thought they were gorgeous. He had no idea back then that he would be dating Perrie a few months later.

CHAPTER 13

CELEBRITY FRIENDS

Niall made his first celebrity friends while performing on *The X Factor* and he has been adding more and more famous phone numbers to his address book ever since. He has always been a fan of Westlife, so when he met them for the first time it was a big moment in his life. He enjoyed messing around with them, and while they were being interviewed behind the scenes on *The X Factor*, Niall impersonated Kian from the group, saying: 'I just think we're [Westlife] the best boy band out there at the moment – apart from One Direction, of course!'

Mark Feehily and Shane Filan from the group asked him about his Botox and Niall replied: 'I've been looking a bit shabby for the last 12 years.'

When Kian turned up, Niall pretended that he had mistaken

him for himself, so he directed him to where Harry, Zayn, Liam and Louis were standing. Kian found Niall so funny.

Westlife had some good advice to give One Direction back then, before they became successful, as Mark explained to *Digital Spy*: 'They need great songs, but they've got a lot of potential to be successful. There are other pop acts who've come out over the last couple of years who don't look as good and don't sing as well, but they've done well because they've had great music.

'They've got a lot of work to do – just natural band work. It only happens through time. They've been put together, so they've got to learn to get on with each other day to day, learn how to like each other and find their positions within the group, and when all that happens, they can really take off.'

***

DID YOU KNOW?

When Niall was younger he used to go to a lot of Westlife concerts and he really loved their music.

***

Other celebrities who rated Niall and the boys when they were on *The X Factor* included Kelly Rowland, Hayden Panettiere, The Saturdays, Alexis Jordan, Lorraine Kelly and Alexandra Burke. Nicole Scherzinger loved them as individuals and as a group, telling journalists gathered at the launch of *The X Factor* 2012: 'It has been crazy to see how massive they are in the US. Just yesterday I was remembering how we put those guys together. It's an incredible feeling to feel like you were part of something like that at the very beginning.' She also joked that she was still waiting for them to give her some flowers for the part she played in putting them together.

One of Niall's closest celebrity friends is Tulisa, who wasn't

a judge when Niall was on the show although she is now. She thinks Niall is one of the most fun people to hang out with as he's always up for having a laugh and has loads of energy. If she's ever feeling down, Niall can put a smile on her face, just by talking to her. They like jamming together as they both love music so much. When Niall had some time off in the summer, they went to V Festival in Chelmsford together. Caroline Flack and Gareth Varey, the *X Factor* judges' PA, came along too and they had a really good time. Tulisa posted photos of them partying on Twitter and the message: 'With @NiallOfficial @carolineflack1 and @GarethVarey in disguise in the crowd! Me n Nial pretending 2b chez n Tom from Sheffield ha #VFest.'

Gareth also posted up some photos of them pouting and pretending to kiss. Niall thoroughly enjoyed himself, partying until 4am with four of his friends from Mullingar and some celebrities in the Hylands Park VIP section. When the last bar closed he went on a 'bus party' with Diana Vickers and actress Billie Piper. They spent time with Ed Sheeran and chatted to Example. According to journalist Clemmie Moodie they had a blast until security put a stop to it. Niall spoke to her the next day, saying: 'I didn't drink too much because I got here quite late on Saturday – I was pretty chilled, really. I was really sweaty in my tent in the morning, though. But it's not really a festival if you don't stay in a tent: you have to camp.'

DID YOU KNOW?

At the V Festival Liam and Louis stayed in a huge tent, which looked like a London Underground tube train.

> #### DID YOU KNOW?
>
> Tulisa's former bandmate and cousin Dappy would love to write a song for One Direction. He told *Digital Spy*: 'They're amazing, they're a breath of fresh air. All of their voices, they've all got individually very unique voices, and yeah, I'd love to sit in a studio with them if they gave me the chance.' Dappy wrote The Wanted's track 'Bring It Home' with Nathan from the band.

A few days after the festival, Niall went to see JLS perform in Brighton and then visited the house of magician and illusionist Dynamo (real name Steven Frayne). They watched TV together, sat next to a giant panda cuddly toy wearing a gas mask, and played pool on Dynamo's customised table. Niall loved it, and posed for a photo lying on the table, smiling and giving the thumbs up. He didn't go to sleep that night until 3am.

> #### DID YOU KNOW?
>
> If Niall could be on any TV show he would pick *I'm A Celebrity... Get Me Out Of Here!* because he would get to live in the Australian jungle. His friend Dougie Poynter from the boy band McFly had been in the 11th series and Niall had asked One Direction fans to vote for him. He had tweeted: 'Everyone! Our boy dougie is in the final of #imaceleb tonight, would be great to see him win, massive achievement, so vote on 09011323203.' The message trended worldwide and Dougie won, beating TOWIE reality star Mark Wright.

Lots of big stars have offered Niall and the other boys advice

because they know what it's like to suddenly become famous. Roger Taylor, the drummer from 80s band Duran Duran, told BBC Radio 5 the advice he would give them now they have been successful in America is: 'Stick with it – the great thing about America is that once they get you, they really get you.'

Duran Duran's lead singer Simon Le Bon added: 'I think that with any band that comes out of something like *The X Factor*, or any of those shows on TV, it's very important for those acts not to just be putty in the hands of the producers.'

Cheryl Cole likes to joke that One Direction are so popular internationally because of her. She told *Sugarscape* (while laughing): 'I took credit for [One Direction] on Twitter – I Twittered the boys, saying, "Remember who really mentored you when Simon [Cowell] wasn't around!"

'There was a couple of weekends where Simon was poorly and I had to mentor them, so I take full responsibility for all their success – and over the pond, I think it's all me.'

Paul McCartney also had some words of wisdom for Niall and the boys when he appeared on the ITV breakfast show *Daybreak*. The Beatles' legend doesn't think the media should constantly compare fans' reactions to One Direction with the reaction The Beatles got in their heyday. 'There are so many bands who all get called "the next Beatles",' he explained. 'Suddenly it puts an awful lot of pressure on them to be the next Beatles.

'Oasis were "the next Beatles" once, if you remember. It's a pressure because suddenly you've got to live up to all the things that we did, and it was a different time. So let's just call them "the next terrific band".'

Niall has spent quite a bit of time with Justin Bieber, but before they met properly Harry joked that he would like to wrestle him. He told the *Daily Record*: 'We could get some sumo suits. And have a wrestling thing.'

Justin thinks that Niall and the other boys are great, telling the *Mirror*: 'We have a lot of fun whenever we hang out. They came over my house and we were just chilling out around the pool and listening to music.' Justin would like to work with them in the future and thinks that their desire to collaborate with Rihanna, Taylor Swift and Jennifer Lopez might be made possible because of the way they look, as well as their voices. 'They sure have an eye for the ladies, but even better for the guys, the ladies have a bit of an eye for them, too,' he said. 'From what I hear they shouldn't have much trouble trying to persuade Rihanna, Katy or Taylor to work with them... if you know what I'm saying.'

Justin doesn't believe Niall and the others will ever get big headed, even though they are right now the biggest band in the world. He thinks their friendships with each other will help them keep their feet on the ground.

CHAPTER 14

HAVING FUN

Niall loves his food and can often be found munching on something just before he is interviewed for a magazine or radio show. They say that the way to a man's heart is through his stomach and this is certainly true for him. Louis thinks that if a girl wants to get Niall's attention she just needs to seduce him with food!

In an interview with 94.7 Fresh FM, Niall was asked what his strategy would be to survive the *Hunger Games*, and he replied: 'I'd give up coz I'd get too hungry early; I'd probably die straight away.'

In the same interview he revealed how he has three sugars in his tea, telling the fan interviewing him, 'Back home we call it a "builder's tea" – it's like really strong tea, loads of milk, loads of sugar so basically you can stand your spoon up in it. It's that strong.'

> **DID YOU KNOW?**
>
> Louis is the only member of One Direction who doesn't have sugar in his tea.

When Niall was a young boy, his mum taught him how to bake cupcakes and they tasted delicious. While One Direction were on *The X Factor* and Niall lived with the other contestants in a house, he had three options: he could cook everything himself, share with someone else or order takeaway. The takeaway option won – because they were spending so much time rehearsing every day Niall often didn't have the energy to cook something when he got in. One Direction would eat burgers, fried chicken, pizzas and Indian meals while they lived there because it was easier. He still loves eating takeaways and will often have them when he's home in London.

> **DID YOU KNOW?**
>
> One day Louis caught Niall trying to put M&M's chocolates in alphabetical order.

When One Direction were in Australia they appeared on the TV show *Sunrise* and had to try lots of different foods. Niall was given some toast with Vegemite spread on it, but when he tasted it he couldn't help but grimace. Thankfully Zayn passed him a napkin so he could spit it out – he thought it was disgusting. He tweeted afterwards: 'Can clearly say vegemite is horrible! Like tryin new stuff though.'

Sunrise decided to auction off Niall's toast to raise money for the Australian charity Youngcare. They put it on eBay with the message: 'The item is perishable and although we will package it so that tampering is evident, we do not advise that it is

consumed. We will not be including the mouthful that Niall spat out — because that's just gross.'

The starting bid was just $0.99 (£0.64) but fans started bidding and soon the price was to $1,000 (£648). By the time bidding ended it was an unbelievable $100,000 (£65,000).

On their flight from Australia back to the UK Niall felt rough, tweeting: 'Not feeling the best! sore all over! under the weather as they say!' Later on he added: 'Food poisoning not good!'

Niall was looking forward to having some time off to chill out. After they landed he tweeted: 'Yessss! Back in london! Sleep for the next week, don't wana see a sole' [sic]. He also sent a message to 'All Night Long' singer Alexandra Burke, saying: 'ari alex..whats crackin? since im gona be soo tired n jetlagged when im home..ur gona havta help me out hahahaha. i joke...Yes burkey, we're back, I cannot wait t sleep.'

Niall hates being jetlagged and tweeted on 2 September 2012: 'I dont like jet lag! He's evil! He just threw a bucket of water over me t wake me up at 6 am!oh no that was a glass of water I spilt #wee.'

Niall's love for food has got him into trouble in the past. When the boys were flying out to America once he nearly missed his flight because he had been having some Japanese food in the airport's Wagamama restaurant with Liam. He loves eating there and once tweeted a photo of three empty plates and an empty bowl with the message: 'Niall VS Food! Haha I win.'

DID YOU KNOW?
If they get ambushed at a restaurant, the boys will sneak out through the kitchen.

Here are Niall's top food tweets:

'Morning all, ya know when ur that hungry ya feel like ur stomach has eaten itself! Another fun day today i think lookin forward t bed tonight.'

'Meself and @zaynmalik are goin for the pot noodle and wotsits days again! love it.'

'Goodmorning! what a day yesterday shooting the video! gona be sick! director is a legend! still in bed now! starvin but cudnt be bothered.'

Niall tweeting about muesli: 'No not never! worst excuse for a breakfast ever! Boooo #rabbitfood.'

'Had soo much mcdonalds this week!'

Niall's other passion is sport, especially football and golf. One Direction enjoy playing football together or watching it on a big TV. They'll play inside or outside, they don't mind, but they take care not to knock anything over if they are playing in their apartments.

In November 2010, while they were appearing on *The X Factor*, they got the chance to meet Man United star Rio Ferdinand when he was launching his new footwear range in Selfridges, London. At the special VIP party they saw JLS, McFly and footballer Jermaine Jenas. Rio came over to talk to them and said that he was a big fan. He invited them to go and see England play France at Wembley the following week. It was a once-in-a-lifetime opportunity but they had to get the okay from Simon Cowell before accepting his kind invitation – they

needed to make sure it wouldn't impact on their performance on the Saturday night.

Simon said they could go and Niall had a great time, even though he was watching England rather than Ireland. They were given free England shirts and sat in the best box in the stadium. Niall apologised for wearing an England shirt, tweeting: 'Great night tonight at Wembley not the best result but met most of the players, went on the pitch got matchballs.

'Sorry Ireland. I wore an English shirt to the game tonight. Got it free and football is football love it. Gonna get my dad t bring Irish 1.'

Louis told the official *X Factor* site afterwards: 'It was amazing! We just lived out every schoolboy's fantasy and chatted to the players as if they were mates. When we left, we were given the actual match balls they played with!

'It was a magical night capped off by going out onto the Wembley pitch when all the fans had gone home. You got a tingle thinking about all the brilliant players that had played there. We asked if we could have a kick-around but they said no!'

Before they left the stadium they were interviewed on FA TV and the presenter asked if they'd be wearing their England shirts on Saturday's *X Factor*. Niall replied: 'Not a chance!' They were also asked what team they supported: Niall said he supported Derby, Liam said Arsenal, and Harry, Zayn and Louis all said Manchester United. The boys also revealed that Simon Cowell used to support United but isn't a football fan anymore.

Niall has been to see many more football mates since, and is invited to the Players Lounges afterwards.

DID YOU KNOW?

Niall has a dodgy knee. He revealed how he got it in an interview with the *Sun*: 'I dislocated my knee playing

football one time,' he said. 'When I got checked by the specialist I was told I've got a 67 per cent chance of walking down the street and my knee dislocating itself.'

In October 2012 Niall had to use crutches after damaging his knee. He explained to Capital FM what happened: 'A squirrel attacked me – I got attacked in Battersea Park. They're dangerous; it's rare. I've torn most of the ligaments in my knee so no football for me.

'It's early retirement now. I've got a floating knee-cap.'

He was told that he would need two and a half months of rehab to fix his knee – poor Niall!

* * *

For Niall's 18th birthday, on 13 September 2011, his parents flew over from Ireland to London to see him, but he also went partying with Liam, Louis and Zayn. Poor Harry was still 17, so he couldn't join them because they were going clubbing. Niall wore a white T-shirt, blue trousers, green pumps and a navy trench coat; he looked gorgeous. His celebrity friends came along too – there was actor/comedian James Corden, JLS and The Saturdays. They started off in the bar of the Sanderson hotel and then went on to the clubs Movida and Chinawhite. It was a joint celebration with Liam, whose birthday had been two weeks earlier.

When Liam turned 19 he had a party at the Funky Buddha club in Mayfair. Niall was running a bit late and tweeted: 'Why is traffic in london soo bad? Soo frustratin, haha also taxi driver loves classical music, smashin it up! Never heard so many symphonies.' He arrived at the club

with One Direction's supporting band, but the bouncer didn't recognise him and wasn't going to let him in at first. Eventually, Niall was allowed in and he partied with Harry. Liam's girlfriend at the time, Danielle Peazer, also threw him a party at the All Star Lane bowling in London, with a batman-themed cake.

For his 19th birthday party, Niall hosted a charity golf day and charity dinner in Mullingar with Boyzone star Keith Duffy. On the morning of his birthday he tweeted: 'look out the window..see rain! perfect weather for golf....naaaatttt.'

'I just woke up! I'm 19 wohoooo! Thank you all so much for the birthday wishes and stuff! love u.'

'Lovely voice note from @justinbieber @DannyRiach @ZaynMalik @AlfredoFlores wishing me happy birthday. Love those dudes! Xxxx.' (Danny Riach is Zayn's friend and Alfredo Flores is a director and friend of Justin Bieber.)

His brother Greg was going to see him at the golf but he still tweeted: 'Just wanna wish my bro @NiallOfficial happy 19th birthday and hope he knows how proud I am of him I remember the day he was born the best'.

Here are Greg's top tweets:

'Mullingar has 2 Olympic medals both Olympics and a brit award and 3 vma's so proud of my bro I could cry I live him too bits and all 1D.'

'Guys I'm so thankful for all the follows on this wow mind blowing x x x x love u guys x x x.'

'yee lot love me I'm not looking for fame it's just crazy how yee guys r about my bro it's cool yee make my day every day.'

'proud is an understatement he hasn't a clue how much I love him and am proud of him he has his dream I'm happy.'

'@NiallOfficial congrats bro on the us number 1 I'm proud of u.'

'I'm going tour on tuesday guys can't wait 1d all the way.'

'Happy new year too all yer 1d crew let's make one direction the biggest spoken about topic in the world in 2012 x x.'

Here are niall's best random tweets:
'I just seen this dude walkin around where I live, headphones on, absolutely dancing away to himself, doin the dougie in the street!'

'still in bed at half 2,well the real reason im still in bed is coz all my boxers are dirty and if i stay in bed,i dont havta change them.'

Before the golf started they visited two local charities: Autism Action and T.E.A.M. (Temporary Emergency Accommodation Mullingar). It was surreal for Niall because he had been a spectator at one of Keith Duffy's charity golf days in the past. He explained to the *Irish Sun* that back then he had begged Keith to let him carry his clubs: 'It's hard to believe but that's what happened four years ago. Keith let me caddy for him and it was weird when he told me he was putting this on and putting my name to it this year. I couldn't believe it.' After Niall had finished being Keith's caddy he was paid €50. Keith remembers him as being very cheeky back then.

Keith Duffy tweeted photos so fans could see what they were up to all day and was full of praise for Niall, tweeting:

'Giving the day of his birthday up for charity and people less fortunate, FAIR PLAY TO YOU NIALL.'

As part of the charity dinner, there was an auction and Niall gave away a signed pair of his boxers for over €200. He modelled a pair of John Joe Nevin's boxing gloves, which went for over €350. That night they stayed up until 6.30am, with Niall singing loads of songs, including the classic Beatles' track 'Twist and Shout'. Irish rock and indie band The Coronas were there, as was *The Voice of Ireland* finalist Conor Quinn.

His mum Maura admitted in an interview in September 2012 she can't believe it's been 19 years since Niall was born, and that he is a huge star. She finds it strange seeing him on TV because he is her little boy. She was so glad she could help him celebrate his birthday in Ireland.

After Niall landed back in London, he tweeted: 'Back in london, had great time at home, love that town! Thanks for the amazing welcome home and for helping me have an amazing birthday.'

Niall is so proud of his Irish roots and makes sure he celebrates St Patrick's Day wherever he is in the world on 17 March every year. In 2012 he tweeted: 'Happy st.patricks day! Cmon the irish #happypaddysday.' He is so grateful to every single fan for supporting him and the boys – and can't wait to see what the future will bring.

Why don't you flip over the book and read *Harry Styles: The Biography...*?